BATTLE FOR ISRAEL

Battle for Israel

Lance Lambert

KINGSWAY PUBLICATIONS
EASTBOURNE

ISBN 0 902088 88 2

Printed in Great Britain for
KINGSWAY PUBLICATIONS LTD,
Lottbridge Drove, Eastbourne, East Sussex BN23 6NT by
Richard Clay (The Chaucer Press) Ltd, Bungay, Suffolk

Contents

Introduction

Israel expected the Day of Atonement* on Saturday, October 6th, 1973, to be as quiet as usual. It was not. It saw the beginning of the most serious of Israel's wars and the fact that at the time many regarded it as just another Arab–Israeli squabble raises two questions. Would it have mattered if Israel had lost and what is the importance and significance of the State of Israel?

I had always found the American Colony Hotel one of the most gracious places in Israel and a friend and I were thoroughly enjoying the last few days of our holiday. It had been the most peaceful one that we had spent in Israel and we had particularly noticed how relaxed everybody was, including the Arab population in Jerusalem and on the West Bank. Our return flight to England was booked for the following Monday in two days' time.

Suddenly air raid sirens wailed all over the city. Although my immediate reaction was to wonder whether this signalled the holiest part of the Day of Atonement, I quickly realized that this could not be the case because the strict laws for Sabbaths and holy days would normally have ruled out the use of sirens. While I was still pondering this, the sirens wailed again. Israel's fourth war had begun.

On the Bar-Lev line along the Suez Canal a bored Jerusalem Brigade swatted flies and slept. Many men were keeping the fast; others were playing a gentle game of soccer when someone kicked the ball to the top of a bulldozed rampart of sand and a private went after it. Looking out over the Canal, he was shocked by what he saw. 'MIGs! MIGs!' he shouted, as Israel came under attack from two hundred Egyptian fighters.

On the Golani Heights, eighty Israeli soldiers were

*See Appendix.

enjoying a day of leisurely military duty. Some were still playing backgammon in their slippers when four Syrian helicopters filled with assault troops swooped round a mountain. Many Israelis were killed in hand-to-hand fighting in the bunkers; others surrendered, only to be executed.

Israel had become overconfident since her last confrontation with her hostile neighbours, and she was taken by surprise. With the Arabs united for the first time for many centuries, equipped with the latest weapons and confident of victory, it appeared that this tiny nation with such a rich religious heritage would be destroyed. Another act in the unfolding drama of the battle for Israel had begun. This was the Yom Kippur War.

1. Annihilation Averted

The Yom Kippur War should have been the annihilation of the State of Israel.

People think of the 1967 Six Day War as a miracle, but it was nothing compared with the Yom Kippur War and in the years that lie ahead, when the whole truth comes out, we shall see that it was beyond all reason that Israel was not annihilated.

A few weeks after the war, I heard Golda Meir say, 'For the first time in our twenty-five year history, we thought we might have lost.' Before then I had never heard a prominent Israeli so much as imply the possibility of defeat or admit to fear. At one point in the war, only ninety battered Israeli tanks stood between the powerful Egyptian army and Tel Aviv, yet Israel was not beaten.

The Yom Kippur War of October 1973 marked a new point in world history, and things will never be the same again. Another such turning point was the First World War when a whole order of things passed away, and the face of Europe and the world was changed, much more than with the Second World War, which only finished off the process. Kingdoms and monarchies disappeared, new ideologies arose, and Marxism had its birth in that era. In a similar way the Yom Kippur War, far from being some petty Middle East fracas, was one of the great milestones of history.

Yom Kippur is a Hebrew name and means 'Day of Atonement'. Among Latin and Oriental Jews (the Sephardim) this Jewish holy day is also called 'the Day of Judgment'. On this day Jews pray particularly for forgiveness, and ask God that their names be 'written and sealed into the Book of the Living.'*

On the Day of Atonement everything in Israel is at a

*See Appendix.

9

standstill. From two hours before sunset until two hours after the succeeding sunset everything stops. There is no transport: no taxis, cars, buses, planes, trains, or ships. The nation's airports are closed, the ports are closed and the stations are closed. No shops are open, and no entertainment can be had anywhere. There are no radio programmes, no television; no communication with the outside world, and very little within Israel. Even the telephone exchanges are not staffed on the Day of Atonement. It is a day of prayer and fasting, spent either in the synagogue or at home.

Israeli Intelligence knew all about troop movements in both Egypt and Syria, but had misinterpreted the signs. These two countries held military manoeuvres in September and October every year and therefore General Dayan along with the Israeli Cabinet thought that these troop movements were just a war of nerves, a bluff designed to produce another Israeli mobilization with the accompanying paralysis of the economy and tremendous financial drain. Only in June that year a general Israeli mobilization cost the country £4,000,000 per day and tore over a third of the manpower out of the economy.

Moreover Israel thought of Anwar Sadat, the President of Egypt, as a 'weak sister' and was confident that the Arabs lacked the unity that was essential for mounting an organized attack. So the possibility of a new war was recognized two weeks before it actually began and the Minister of Defence and government officials later admitted they knew of enemy concentrations but could not accept the verdict of immediate war. Shimon Peres then Minister of Transport and present Minister of Defence said, 'We did not want to believe our own intelligence; we did not want to believe that Sadat was going to attack.' It was four o'clock in the morning on the Day of Atonement before it was realized that something very serious was afoot.

A United Nations representative, who had already passed on highly accurate information to his Israeli counterpart informed him that in the course of the Day of Atonement, Israel would be attacked on two fronts. This warning was taken extremely seriously when it was finally relayed to Israel but by then it was too late. It takes at least forty-eight hours for a full mobilization of the Israeli defence forces. By seven o'clock that morning the military authorities had started to recall men from leave but it was only two hours before the war began that most of the men were contacted and the reserves mobilized.

In this particular year the Day of Atonement was more generally kept than ever before. A large number of the men on the fronts were actually observing the fasting and prayer, and all over the country synagogues were filled with people, mostly men.

Our first public warning that something was wrong came when the air raid sirens wailed for about three minutes at ten past two in the afternoon and again at twenty past two. Within fifteen minutes Israeli radio was on the air broadcasting live reports from both fronts. You could hear gunfire and explosions in the background. These sirens were in fact, the only means the Israeli Government had of informing the nation that something very serious had happened. Husbands and fathers, brothers and sons were suddenly called from synagogue or home with only a few minutes to say good-bye to their families. The majority of them thought it was a short skirmish such as they had had before. They left hurriedly fully expecting to come back, but three thousand of them never returned, and thousands more were maimed for life.

The onslaught on both fronts was massive and terrible. There were more tanks on the Syrian front than in the 1941 German offensive against Russia which was two hundred miles long and involved 1,000 tanks. On the Syrian front, the Golani Heights, there were 1,200 tanks on a twenty-mile front and later at Sinai were fought the greatest tank battles in world history, greater even than the battle of El Alamein in the Second World War.

In Britain we are at times somewhat imperialistic in our attitude, for instance we have tended to think of Syria as a tinpot Middle East state which could be flattened by a single blow. Syria however in that initial attack hit Israel with more tanks than Britain and France possessed between them. Indeed one high-ranking English officer in a tank regiment told me that as of now Britain and France have only one-third of their tanks actually ready for use in the event of an attack. In the Yom Kippur War which was the first wholly techno-logical war in Middle East history approximately 4,000 tanks, 900 missile batteries and even unproved new weapons were thrown into action. Abba Eban, former Foreign Minister of

Israel said in his statement to the United Nations on October 8th, 1973: 'Egypt attacked with 3,000 tanks, 2,000 heavy guns, 1,000 aircraft, and 600,000 men.'

The regular Israeli garrisons numbered only a few hundred men against Syria's massive tank attack. With their greater numbers the Egyptians should have been in El Arish if not in Gaza and Beersheba, within twenty-four hours and then the whole of Israel's heartland would have been exposed. There was nothing to stop them. The U.S. Pentagon estimated that Israel was technologically superior and therefore did not need to be comparably equipped so she was not armed to the same extent as her Arab neighbours.

It turned out that the Arabs however had not only more weapons but often better weapons than the Israelis. They used hand-held missiles such as the RPG7 which can blow the turret right off a tank and the Snapper, a mobile anti-tank rocket which makes tanks burn so fiercely that the armour melts. They also had SAM 6s (surface to air missiles), anti-aircraft rockets that travel at two and a half times the speed of sound. At six miles range this gives a pilot only a matter of seconds in which to take evasive action, so in the early stages of the war three out of every five Israeli jets were shot down. In those first few days Israel suffered terrible casualties.

The Bar-Lev line fell, the Hermon fortress, which most people had thought of as invincible, was taken. Then the Egyptians crossed into Sinai, and the Syrians took much of the Golan. Until this happened the Israeli news service had always been most reliable and many Arabs tuned into Israeli Arabic broadcasts for accuracy. During the first week of the war however, Israeli news tended to be very inaccurate and news from Damascus and Cairo much more dependable.

This was largely due to a breakdown in communications between the front and second lines of defence on the Israeli side. Even Moshe Dayan was confused on the second day of the war because of this. Whole companies and units were wiped out without a survivor. Yet on the whole morale on the Israeli side was very high, especially at the front.

Egypt and Syria should have beaten Israel, but they were inexplicably prevented. The Egyptian high command gave the first Egyptian division that crossed the Canal fifteen hours to take the Bar-Lev line. They took it in just five hours, and then halted. If they had swept on, the whole of central Israel would have been at their mercy. One Egyptian tank commander said later, 'I was only half an hour's drive from the Mitla Pass, and there was nothing to stop me.' Yet the fact is he stopped.

Likewise the Syrians should have been in Tiberias on the evening of the first day of the war but they too stopped. The commanding officer of Israel's Golani brigade said later in my presence that when the Syrians were first advancing, the Israelis had only two tanks and ten men at their NAFAQ headquarters. This man held no religious belief, but he referred to this as a miracle. Although he had been involved in the four previous wars of Israel's history he had never seen anything like it. Wave after wave of tanks bore down on them. Then when they came to within one mile of the NAFAQ head-quarters, they halted. 'They saw the Lake of Galilee,' he said, 'they liked the view, and they stopped.'

As a result of these delays in the Egyptian and Syrian advance Israel had time to regroup and reorganize. Many think that it was this period of time that made all the difference to the outcome of the Yom Kippur War.

Another Israeli captain without any religious beliefs said that at the height of the fighting on the Golan, he looked up into the sky and saw a great, grey hand pressing downwards as if it were holding something back. In my opinion that describes exactly what happened; without the intervention of God, Israel would have been doomed.

Shimon Peres, once a key adviser to Golda Meir and at present Minister of Defence, has said, 'The miracle is that we ever win. The Arab nations occupy eight per cent of the surface of the world. They possess half the known oil resources and are immensely rich. They have more men in their armies than we have people in our state, and in addition the Russians have built for them a great war machine. On our side we have only America.'

It was at this point in the war that I first learned of the massive Soviet airlift of arms to Syria and Egypt which had begun on the first day of the war. Two hours after the war started Antonov transport planes carrying weapons and replacements were landing every three minutes and at the same time that the war began, Russian ships arrived at Latakia, Syria and Alexandria, Egypt, carrying heavy military replacements for everything that would be lost in the fighting. Three days before the war began the Soviet Union had launched two orbital Sputniks which crossed Israel at the best time for aerial photography. Russia then relayed information to Syria and Egypt as to whether Israel was prepared. This is probably why the war originally planned for six o'clock in the evening of Yom Kippur, was brought forward to two o'clock. The Russians had passed on the information that preparations had begun on the Israeli side. Others have suggested that it may have been the result of a compromise between the Syrians who wanted to launch the attack at six a.m. with the sun behind them and the Egyptians who wanted the attack to commence at six p.m.

The American airlift with each plane carrying a hundred tons of ammunition, tanks and weapons did not begin until the tenth day of the war when the Israeli army was actually running out of ammunition. The delay was caused almost completely by the refusal of America's so-called allies, particularly Britain, to grant facilities to the United States for refuelling her planes. Britain was so bitter about the airlift that she persuaded her NATO allies to fight it. Germany refused to allow the United States to take weapons from her bases on German soil and put them on Israeli ships in Bremen and Hamburg. Eventually Portugal opened up the Azores to United States transport planes and Israel was saved. Planes then came in almost nose to tail; there was no time to lose. If they had not come, Israel would have been totally lost.

The fighting became increasingly severe. Galilee was shelled and the Syrians even used Frog missiles. There were many air raids in the north but then Syria was gradually pushed back. Meanwhile, Egypt was held in the Sinai where the greatest tank battle in world history was fought on Friday, October 19th. Much of the fighting was at such close range that they weren't even able to manoeuvre the tanks. Jordanian radio described it as 'Hell on earth'.

Although the British and French embargo on arms was supposed to be even handed, it was in fact loaded against Israel.

I have seen for myself some of the many British weapons captured by the Israeli defence forces. Presumably they were coming from Kuwait into Syria because Britain supplied Kuwait with arms throughout the war.

Israeli British-made Centurion tanks were immobilized

through lack of ammunition and spare parts. Due to the urgency of the situation some tanks which went to the front under their own power rather than waiting to be transported had damaged their tracks by the time they arrived there. Spare parts and ammunition had already been paid for but as they were on board Israeli ships in British ports when the embargo was placed on them, the entire cargo was impounded by the British Government. There would certainly have been an outcry in Britain if India, for example had taken the same action with ships flying the British flag.

Two French Mirage fighters were shot down and captured by Israel; yet there are only two nations in the Mediterranean which use Mirages — Israel and Libya. Libya, supposedly non-belligerent was supplied by France with planes and weapons throughout the war. It seems that she passed on this equipment to Egypt. The French embargo on Israel moreover was so bitter that France did not even allow blood donated by French volunteers to be sent to the Israeli wounded.

Many nations joined Egypt and Syria. In the first twelve days Saudi Arabia, Kuwait, Yemen, Iran, Sudan, Libya, Morocco, Algeria, Tunis and Jordan all came in on the Arab side and North Vietnam sent a contingent of pilots to Syria. In the first two weeks of the war, twenty-seven African states broke off relations with Israel yet many of them had been the recipients of Israeli aid. Thirty-four states in all including India, broke off relations. Other countries which were supposed to be impartial such as Malta, were in fact bitterly hostile to Israel at this time.

So Israel became increasingly isolated. People sometimes wonder how Armageddon* could ever take place. This war showed that within a few days contingents from all the armies of the world could be in Israel.

Israel's isolation also occurred on another front. With the exception of the Moderator of the Church of Scotland, no church leader condemned the fact that the war was a premeditated attack on the most sacred day in the Jewish calendar. If anything was said faintly resembling condemnation, it was qualified with remarks sympathetic to the Arab cause. The Israeli Cabinet felt very bitter about this. Some of them said 'We never expected Christian churches to support us in the war, nor would we ever expect Christian churches to

*See Appendix.

collect money for ammunition or weapons. We did not even expect them to collect money for our wounded. But we thought that the least they could do was to stand up and say that they thought it was a terrible thing that on the most sacred and holy day of the Jewish calendar, when everyone was fasting and praying, this premeditated attack took place.'

The Pope just talked about the need for peace on both sides and said that one could not blame the Arabs for longing for their old homelands. It is a sad fact that the Vatican has not yet recognized Israel as a sovereign state. The World Lutheran Federation remained absolutely silent as did the Anglican Church. The World Council of Churches sent over a million pounds' worth of aid to Jordan and an undisclosed sum to the Palestinians. These funds were for the relief of war victims on the Arab side and for the refugee programme amongst the Palestinians. Some of this money could well have found its way to the terrorists. Until this time not even a penny had been sent to Israel but owing to criticism that they were not being even-handed, the Council committed themselves to sending five and a half tons of medical supplies to Israel.

It has to be understood that the World Council of Churches has in its membership many churches in the Arab world and consequently there are numerous requests for help sent to Geneva from there. On the other hand there is no similar organization in Israel to seek assistance. Then there are the very definite leftist and radical tendencies of the Third World majority in the Central Committee of the Council. It is because of these tendencies that its members side with the Arabs against Israel.

In the recent Nairobi conference of the World Council of Churches some of these issues came to the surface. The General Secretary, Dr Phillip Potter, publicly professed his ineradicable prejudice against white people and even accused Britain of being 'responsible for the most racist system in history'. There were also a number of complaints made about the double standards adopted by the Council, notably that they were 'operating one law for the Right and another for the Left.' One of the most respected of British churchmen and Parliamentarians, Sir Cyril Black, as a result of that conference wrote to the Daily Telegraph calling upon British churches 'to consider carefully whether they can any longer, in good conscience, continue in membership of the World Council of Churches'.

Furthermore Israel appears to have suffered ostracism from the International Red Cross, for this body recognizes the Red Crescent of the Arabs and the Red Lion and Sun of the Iranians and at the same time refuses recognition to the Red Shield of David (Magen David Adom). Until 1975 it seems that the leadership of this well-known organization did not think it appropriate to give attention to the case of such recognition probably because of the well known political difficulties in which they would be involved. Now it is due to be considered and it will be interesting to see the outcome of their deliberations. To the onlooker it must seem strange that while other national or religious symbols are acceptable, the Jewish symbol is not. Again in a Red Cross congress held in the late autumn of 1973 a vote of censure on Israel's conduct of the war received a two-thirds majority.

While one feels that this does not really represent the true policy of the leadership of the International Red Cross it does reveal the problems such an organization faces in dealing with new states, particularly Israel.

Many of the Christians in Jerusalem felt that the main purpose of my being delayed there was for prayer. We had been staying at the American Colony Hotel but after two weeks it was becoming too costly. It was at that crucial moment that the then warden of the Garden Tomb, Jan Willem van der Hoeven and his wife offered us accommodation in a house at the Garden Tomb. Many believe that the site of the Garden is the place of the resurrection of Christ. It was as if one was at the heart of things. Here was the natural centre for most of the Christians in Jerusalem: My burden was that among them there should be a ministry of genuine corporate prayer. I found here as everywhere else, that this was a lost art. So many Christians know how to pray on their own but they do not know how to pray together.

I was appalled that when Israel was in such great need, even Christian workers and servants of the Lord who had been clearly put there by God and really felt God calling them to pray for all that was going on at that time, were unable to pray together in depth. This was not because these Christians were necessarily divided on personal or doctrinal issues, neither was it due to any lack of private devotion nor godliness. The reason was that the art of praying together has been largely lost. So we held a school of prayer at the height of the war. Our burden was for the dying and wounded, Arab and Jew alike, that they might be saved; for the Israeli people, that the war might be used to turn them to God; for the invaders, that the Lord would paralyse and confuse them and especially for Jordan, that she would not enter the war.

A member of our group with a military background, a typical Britisher not given to fantasy – came to me and said that on the third day of the war a picture came to his mind when he was praying. He saw himself on the Mount of Olives. He saw great clouds roll out of heaven down on to the Mount of Olives and from there across the wilderness of Judea, blotting out the whole country of Jordan. It was so vivid that he immediately turned in prayer to the Lord and said, 'Lord, what does this mean?' He felt that the Lord replied, 'Pray that the Jordanian authorities will be so confused that they do not enter the war.'

He came to me early the next morning and recounting his experience asked, 'Do you really think that it was of God?' I felt that it was.

We felt quite sure that we must give ourselves to much prayer that clouds would come down upon King Hussein and the Jordanian Cabinet. We also prayed that Christians would be protected and used at both fronts and at home. We had some remarkable answers to our prayers. Jordan stayed out of the war. Officially she sent a token force, a crack regiment called the 40th Brigade. However, the 40th stayed behind a hill on the Syrian front and hardly fired a shot. Indeed one Israeli general felt that they were there to stop the Syrians and Iraqis from entering Jordan rather than to fight the Israelis. The bridges over the river Jordan were open to civilian traffic for almost the whole war, closing on only three separate occasions in the course of four months.

We had the tremendous joy of hearing King Hussein being interviewed in English on a radio broadcast. The Indian interviewer said, 'You are very unpopular with quite a number of the Arab states because they feel that you have let down the Arab cause and that if you had opened the third front, Israel *would* have been finished. Hussein replied, 'Well, they may feel that, and I can understand it. But you see, we were very perplexed the day the war began and ever since, for we do not feel that we have sufficient air cover to allow us to attack. We are not sure that we would have got the support that we needed from Iraq and Syria.' That was a great answer to prayer, and he had even used the word 'perplexed'.

We continued to pray that God would confuse the invaders and cause them to hesitate. We also asked that there might be the miracle of national repentance and prayer. We prayed for the Israeli Cabinet, especially for Golda Meir, then seventy-six years of age. Mrs Meir was an agnostic but at Ben-Gurion's funeral in 1973, she said, 'I thank the Almighty that two years ago he brought about reconciliation between me and David Ben-Gurion.' I had heard her use expressions such as 'Thank God' for this or for that previously, but only as a colloquialism. I had never heard her refer to the Almighty in this way.

Among other things we prayed that the hidden motives and counsels of the Soviet Union might be unmasked before President Nixon and the Free nations and that President Nixon's impeachment at such a time might be averted. We prayed that he would give up the two tapes, although at that time he was resisting this. We prayed that the Egyptian Third Army would be surrounded and even surrender thus bringing a speedy end to the conflict.

We had some remarkable answers to these prayers. For the first time in Israeli history, one of the three leading Rabbis of the Jewish Agency* sent out a letter appealing for repentance on the part of the Jewish people. He listed fifteen reasons for the need of this repentance, including Israeli car driving – if you have experienced this, you will understand why.

To those who would charge me with being anti-Arab in my attitude let me say that I count many Arabs among my dearest friends. Furthermore, in the Yom Kippur War we prayed for the safety and deliverance of those Arab believers who were involved in the fighting, some of them known to us. It was a great joy to me to hear later of one remarkable answer to prayer. One of the first men in the Egyptian Army to cross the Suez Canal is a true Christian, the son of an Egyptian pastor who is one of my dear friends. This young man, a captain in the Engineers, was a leader of a unit of fifteen men. They were to be responsible for the laying of the 'carpet

*See Appendix.

bridges' across the water of the canal. He had understood that
the Egyptian authorities considered that there would be few
survivors among those who were in the forefront of
the battle. Just before the war began he was praying and
opened his Bible at Acts 27:24, and read 'and lo, God hath
granted thee all them that sail with thee.' After the bitter
fighting of those first few days, his unit was the only unit
which came through unscathed. Even more remarkable is the
fact that his half track broke down in the midst of the fiercest
tank battle ever fought in world history. For over half an hour
it lay immobilized between Egyptian and Israeli tanks locked
in battle. He knew that he was a sitting target but was unable
to get out and do anything. Placing himself in God's hands he
told him that he was ready to die if his time had come. Then
when he tried the engine again it started up and he was saved.
I remember so well this young man being prayed for fervently
by name at about the time of this battle.

The Egyptian Third Army was surrounded and cut off and
became dependent upon the Israeli forces for food and
medical supplies. The Israeli army broke through the Egyptian
defences and poured over the Canal into Egypt. Syria was
pushed back to within fifteen miles of Damascus. President
Nixon gave up the two tapes and his impeachment was
averted.

On Sunday, October 21st, Kissinger was urgently called to
Moscow by the Kremlin. The next day there was an unofficial
cease-fire on the Suez front, which we felt could be to Israel's
grave disadvantage. For previously, under cover of the 1971
cease-fire, the Soviet Union had supported the moving up of
SAMs by Egypt to within one mile of the Suez Canal. These
ground to air missiles which were not taken away in spite of
much fuss and bother in the United Nations, nearly determined the course of this war.

Why was it that Britain and France did not immediately
forward a motion in the Security Council calling for a cease-
fire when Egypt and Syria moved on to Israeli-held soil?
Evidently President Nixon had personally asked the then
Prime Minister of Britain, Mr Heath, if he would do so but Mr
Heath had refused. True the British Ambassador in Cairo, Sir
Philip Adams, did ask Sadat on October 12th if he would like
a standstill cease-fire on existing positions, by which time the
Egyptian army had crossed the canal, taken the Bar-Lev line

and were advancing towards the Sinai passes. Sadat however refused as the Egyptian army was planning a big offensive the next day and hoped for further territorial gains. The matter was left there despite the fact that at that time Israel was on the verge of defeat. As soon as Damascus and Cairo were threatened however, Britain moved with amazing speed in order to get a cease-fire resolution passed. We prayed that the case-fire might be broken if it was only going to allow Egypt and Syria to rearm and regroup for more bloodshed.

A retired colonel in the Israeli army who was a sabra, a native Israeli, told me 'I have lived here all my life. Every time we have had one of these cease-fires they have not kept it. We report it and report it and report it and then we just have to fight back. That is what will happen this time. They will probably break it three times and the fourth time we will retaliate and take all the territory we need.' That is exactly what happened, the Egyptians broke this unofficial cease-fire three times. On the fourth occasion, the Israelis fought back. They went as far as Ismailia and then turned southwards cutting off Suez City and ending up only fifty miles from Cairo. This made Russia furious. Brezhnev sent Nixon what Senator Henry Jackson in perhaps over-emotional language called 'the most brutal cable ever sent to a President.'

What Brezhnev said in this cable was that the Soviet Union had decided to take unilateral action and so resolve the Israeli problem. America took this very seriously because American reconnaissance flights had already spotted that a large Soviet warship previously seen heading for Alexandria, Egypt, had now docked there. On the deck of this warship were ballistic missiles with nuclear warheads. At the same time the Soviet airlift dramatically stopped and all those huge transport planes were at the ready while crack Soviet parachute regiments moved towards the airfields. Aware of both these facts, President Nixon called a worldwide United States military alert, known as a Stage Three alert in the five-stage American defence Condition. This put 2,300,000 men on stand-by and was the first such alert since the Cuban crisis eleven years before.

Why did the Russians bother to cable Nixon? Why didn't they just get on with the job by letting the Egyptians have a ballistic missile and letting them fire it? Why tell the Americans? According to a high-ranking Israeli expert on

foreign affairs whom I asked about this, the Russians believed
that they must observe some outward form of détente. They
believed that Nixon was in such a domestic crisis that he
would delay at least twenty-four hours, long enough for
Egypt to have fired two or three ballistic missiles and wiped
out Haifa, Tel Aviv and probably western Jerusalem. When it
was over and there was worldwide protest, Russia would hold
up her hands in horror and say 'We are very sorry, but what's
done is done. Israel is finished.' Thank God that in spite of his
personal and national problems, Nixon proved to be quick-
witted and sharp. Whatever the true facts about this matter, it
was certainly more than mere 'sabre rattling' on the part of the
United States and very much more than a cover-up of the
Watergate' scandal. I cannot forget the burden of prayer that
fell upon some of us in Jerusalem on the preceding
day and the urgent and anointed prayer that was made to
God concerning the unmasking of the Soviet Union's plans
and intentions. We were not the only ones to sense the call of
God to pray in this vein.

Samuel Howells, Principal of the Bible College of Wales
and son of Rees Howells the great intercessor, told me later
that one of the greatest times of prayer that he remembers
since the war years came on the night President Nixon called
the alert but before it was publicly known. During that day he
had felt a tremendous burden and anguish come upon him. He
walked up and down, prayed for a while and in the end asked
God 'What does this burden mean?' 'My enemy is seeking to
precipitate Armageddon,' he was told, and Samuel Howells
then spent some time in prayer. Later during the course of a
regular evening meeting he and others felt led by the Holy
Spirit to remain in prayer until early the next day. That
morning they were not surprised to hear about the worldwide
United States military alert although they did not realize the
full situation until I was able to explain it to them some
months later. At approximately the same time thousands of
miles away from Wales, Gladys Thomas and Kitty Morgan
were praying in Israel. They had learned some of the deep
lessons of intercession with Rees Howells, Samuel's father,
during the Second World War. Both of them felt troubled
in spirit throughout the day and as they prayed the Lord had
said to Gladys, 'Pray! For my enemy is seeking to precipitate
the end.' No doubt there were others still unknown to me upon

whom this sense of urgency came as they waited upon the Lord. To such the U.S. worldwide military alert was no surprise.

Throughout the world many thought that the United States alert was ordered for domestic reasons. In fact at that time we came to the very brink of World War Three, though in Britain and the rest of Europe, hardly anyone realized it. We were living in a fool's paradise, teetering on the brink of nuclear war. Christians in the Free World continued their routine meetings and programmes unaware of the grave issues at stake and tremendous movements in the unseen world. The Lord Jesus told us to watch and pray, to be ready for the things coming upon the face of the earth. Were we ready then?

As soon as the United States worldwide military alert was called, the Soviet warship weighed anchor and sailed back to the Black Sea. Israel's annihilation had been averted.

2. How Long Peace?

On November 11th, 1973, the cease-fire was signed. Since then the Arabs have been assiduously involved in a military build-up. By June 1974, military personnel had arrived in the Middle East from Yugoslavia, Russia and other Eastern European countries as well as from North Korea, North Vietnam and Cuba. Their task is to supervise the more sophisticated weapons given to these states by the Soviet Union. For example, seven hundred and fifty Cubans are manning a tank brigade in Syria, and there are over three thousand Russian advisers at operational level in the Syrian armed forces. The Russians are manning ground-to-ground missiles and installing ground-to-air missile-launchers. There are forty-eight North Korean pilots on active duty in the Egyptian air force, and East Germany has sent pilots and electronic warfare specialists.

So Syria has become one vast arsenal and her readiness for war has doubled, or possibly trebled, since October 1973. There is a similar picture when you look at Iraq. Her armed forces have received one thousand T-54 and T-62 tanks, various missiles, including Frog ground to ground missiles, and three hundred and fifty planes, including the new Tupolev 22 long-range bomber. Iraq's forces now have between one thousand and twelve hundred Soviet advisers. There are so many Soviet advisers in Somalia and Aden that through their influence they could actually close down the Bab el Mandeb Straits and so block the whole Red Sea to shipping whenever they wish.

Nor are the Arabs short of money: at the Rabat Conference in October 1974, a fighting fund was set up by the oil-rich Arab states placing £500,000,000 a year at the disposal of Egypt, Syria, Jordan and the Palestinian Liberation Organisation (P.L.O.). Another £35,000,000 per

year was given to South Yemen to establish a major Arab
military base at the Bab el Mandeb Straits.

In the autumn of 1973, Dr Joseph Luns, NATO Secretary-
General and Dutch ex-Foreign Minister, warned the NATO
foreign ministers concerning the Soviet Union's intentions
with these words: 'I feel very much like I did in 1936–37,
watching the Nazi war machine build up while they signed
peace treaties and made pacts taking in most, if not all, of the
governments of Europe.' He went on to warn them:
'Countries do not equip themselves with vast armaments and
devote enormous resources to the acquisition of vast military
strength if they do not contemplate exploiting it.' While the
Warsaw Pact countries and NATO countries have been
talking of forces and weapons reduction, the Soviet Union
and her Eastern European allies have been involved in an
unprecedented military build-up.

The former British Foreign Secretary, Sir Alec Douglas-
Home, patched up a quarrel between Britain and the Soviet
Union over the expulsion of a hundred spies some years ago.
He returned from Moscow however, to tell the same NATO
foreign ministers' conference not to sign a forces and
weapons reduction agreement at the present time. Some light
may be thrown on his attitude by Max van der Stoel, the
present Dutch Minister for Foreign Affairs, who said at the
same conference, 'We have to ask ourselves if the Soviets did
not perhaps put the Arabs up to using the weapon of oil to
undercut the economies of the industrialized West. Indeed we
in NATO have to find out if the Soviets did not instigate the
Arab attack on Israel itself.'

The oil embargo was agreed upon by the Arab oil-
producing states in January 1973, nine months before the war
began. Holland was selected for a total embargo at the same
time. Two-thirds of Western Europe's oil is refined in the port
of Rotterdam, Holland.

In the short term, disengagement seems wonderful; at least
the Israeli prisoners have come back from Syria, and the
Syrian prisoners have returned to their families. It has meant
that war has ceased, the shooting has stopped, and lives are
not being lost. However, it is in fact a short-term peace and a
long-term escalation and in my personal view is therefore a
tragedy.

I was in Israel during the whole course of the disengagement talks with Syria when Kissinger was flying every day to Damascus from Jerusalem and then back again in the evening and at one point it seemed that the whole thing would break down. Russia had an interest in preventing the disengagement from succeeding, mainly because the United States, caught as she was in the middle, wanted it. The United States has been working over-time to get Egypt, Jordan and Syria into her camp and away from Russia's. She must support Israel because of the large and powerful Jewish population in America. Yet she cannot afford to be anti-Arab because of her growing need for Middle East oil and her £1,500,000,000 investment in Arab oil production.

Even if Israel withdrew from her present borders, while the Arab world is still aligned with Russia, a third world war would seem to be inevitable, because the United States would have to guarantee the Israeli frontiers and the Soviet Union the Arab frontiers. There would then be the real possibility of a super-power confrontation. The Americans are fully aware of this, and they are putting colossal pressure on the Israeli Cabinet to withdraw, which means that they know they would have to guarantee Israel's boundaries. The motive has been to entice Egypt, Syria and Jordan into the American camp, as well as Israel. This would enable them to act as guarantor to both the Israelis and the Arabs, rather than having the Russians on one side and themselves on the other.

It is reasonably clear so far that Dr Kissinger is succeeding in getting Egypt into the American camp. Syria however, is another matter, as is Jordan at the present time. The Soviet Union tried to disrupt the disengagement talks and rumour has it that there were two assassination attempts on Kissinger while he was in Damascus. It is widely believed in Israeli government circles that these were the result of Russian KGB activities.

I believe it would be self-deception to think that this disengagement is the first step in peace. Israel has lost every advantage that she so dearly fought for with the lives of her sons. The disengagement zone in the Golan is so narrow, that the Syrians can fire right over the United Nations forces into Israel.

It is, however, Mount Hermon, the most strategic military strongpoint in the whole of the north that Israel was so anxious to control. From its summit you can see the whole of the road to Damascus and you have not only a commanding view of the Golani Heights and all Southern Lebanon but also all of upper Galilee and on a clear day all military manoeuvres can be spotted from this peak. Israel was particularly interested therefore in regaining the Mount Hermon fortress and all three peaks of Hermon. Before the Yom Kippur War Israel held the lower two peaks, but not the highest which actually overlooks Damascus. This she obtained through bitter fighting; indeed, relatively more men were lost in the battle for the Hermon peak than in any other campaign in the war. In the disengagement however, the Hermon peak was taken away from Israel and went under United Nations control. This is a pathetic position for Israel because the Syrians could now build military posts all around the United Nations area of control. Then all Syria would have to do would be to order the United Nations out and the United Nations would have to go. They cannot hold the area.

There are a number of other disadvantages to the cease-fire. Syria for example refused to guarantee officially that terrorists would not act against Israel from Syria. Understandably it was felt in Israel that if Syria really wanted peace, she would have guaranteed this. Then why did Israel agree to a cease-fire with such humiliating disadvantages for her? An Israeli expert on foreign affairs whom I asked about the Hermon peak, said that it was a total waste of life as indeed all the loss of life on the Golan front. I then asked him, 'Isn't it better to keep fighting, rather than agree to something which is so much to your disadvantage?' He replied 'No, we cannot do anything else, because of the pressure that Kissinger is putting on us.'

Kissinger, although he later denied it, implied that the United States would withhold economic aid unless Israel was prepared to withdraw from 'occupied territory'. This is why Israel agreed to give back the Hermon peak, to withdraw from Syria and for the first time to give up territory already claimed by Israeli settlers on the Golan, that is the El Quneitra triangle. El Quneitra which was once the centre for the whole of the Golan is now a ghost town. Under the terms of the agreed disengagement, Syria was to resettle the civilian population in Quneitra. Only sixteen civilians have been allowed to return and that appears ominous to Israel.

Syria is not satisfied. She wants back all of the Golan.

Many have accused the old Israeli Cabinet of a tactical error in giving back El Quneitra because it means that Israel has now no more ground to hand back. If she surrenders any more, the whole of Galilee will be at the mercy of Syria. From the Golan Heights she could then fire down upon all the settlements in Northern Galilee. At the present time therefore Israel considers Syria the real threat rather than Egypt.

It is widely believed that Egypt wants peace at least far more than Syria does, because she has reopened the Suez Canal. She wants to make Port Said a great tourist centre and the civilian population has already begun to return. From January 1st, 1976, Port Said has been declared a tax free haven to encourage foreign investment. Furthermore both Ismailia and Suez are being rebuilt and resettled. Egypt has even condemned some forms of Arab terrorism for the first time. She may therefore really mean what she has said about ending hostilities. Moreover Israel is in a better position to negotiate with Egypt about Sinai as there is much more of Sinai which Israel is prepared to surrender to Egypt than there is of the Golan to give back to Syria. As things are now if Syria demands that she move back, Israel is almost forced to refuse. That is why she gave priority to talks with Egypt, in order to avoid a confrontation with Syria.

We are beginning to see a very interesting re-grouping in the Middle East. Egypt and Saudi Arabia are gradually moving together into a block which is for peace on certain terms. Certainly Egypt is moving towards the American sphere of influence, and away from the Russian. On the other hand, Syria, Iraq, Libya and the Palestinian Liberation Organization are becoming more and more adamant in their demands and have moved further into the Soviet camp, while Jordan and the Lebanon have become unwilling partners with them. It is interesting to note the change of policy in Jordan. King Hussein wisely kept Jordan out of the Yom Kippur War but his influence and prestige suffered as a result. In the Spring of 1975 he began what he publicly called 'the panic buying of arms'. Having been ruled out as the representative of the Palestinian people, he realized that in the next round of fighting he must play a practical role. Since the U.S.A. was somewhat reluctant to supply him with all the arms he wanted, he has now turned to the Soviet Union for military help and aid and Syria and Jordan have set up a united military high command. Furthermore the whole Jordanian frontier with Israel has been prepared for war. Israel has taken this new Jordanian policy very seriously and has responded by preparing defences along her entire border. King Hussein's dilemma is sad. He does not want war, yet he is being forced to compromise and to go to war in any renewed fighting. The Lebanese dilemma is even more sad. Having played with fire Lebanon herself is being burned. She allowed her country to become the springboard for many P.L.O. actions against Israel and now finds herself well-nigh powerless to cope with the Marxist minority bent on the destruction of her country as a Christian—Arab state. In 1975, in ten months of civil war, ten thousand Lebanese have died. By now the number of dead may well have doubled. Twenty-two thousand have been wounded and three thousand six hundred businesses in the capital alone have been destroyed. It will take years for Lebanon to recover to the kind of state she was and in the meantime Syria and the P.L.O. both emerge with a stronger influence over the Lebanon than ever before.

Could Israel have won the Yom Kippur War? I do not think that the Israeli defence forces ever thought that it would be feasible to take either Damascus or Cairo. The reason of course, is that it would take a large number of men to govern such antagonistic populations. At the same time, the general feeling was that Israel was robbed of a decisive victory by Kissinger's diplomacy, for the Israelis had the Egyptians on the run and surrounding them and bringing them to surrender would have meant a decisive victory. Kissinger believed, however, that Arab pride would only make such a humiliating blow the ground for further war.

Both sides consider it a grave possibility that the war will be resumed. King Hussein, interviewed on the BBC at the beginning of 1975, solemnly warned that unless the lost momentum for peace is quickly regained, war is inevitable and would be a disaster for the whole world. The Israeli Prime Minister, Yitzhak Rabin said in the Spring of 1975 'We must expect the resumption of war from the north, that is from Syria.' Probably the first sign will be that Syria will order the United Nations out of the buffer zone. Israel's new policy appears to be that the moment that happens, she will make a pre-emptive strike. Of course that would incur the wrath of the Third World and much of the Western World.

What will Israel do about the missile problem which caused her to lose so many planes in the Yom Kippur War? I am not a technical expert, but I understand that a number of Israeli planes have been fitted with a new chiming device to track incoming missiles. We must remember that the Yom Kippur War very quickly became a trial run for a third world war. The Soviet Union began to send in all kinds of new weapons in order to try them out under conditions of actual war. Even the Pentagon did not know of the existence of some of these. One example, is the latest SAM missiles which have no equivalent in the West. Another is the mines in the Gulf of Suez which neither the American and British navies nor the Israeli navy, were able to neutralize. They had to call in the Soviet navy to do this, because the West has no equivalent mines. The Yom Kippur War was therefore a kind of testing ground for new weapons.

Along with the other problems confronting Israel is the spectre of insolvency. It cost Israel up to one hundred million pounds sterling for every day between October 6th and November 11th, 1973, and since then around four million pounds for every day of general mobilization. The threat of renewed war and continual terrorist activity both outside and inside Israel have reduced her tourist earnings which are her most important means of gaining foreign currency. Moreover the new-found Arab wealth is influencing not only the many nations of the Third World, but the elder nations of the West also. According to an expert's report submitted to a foreign relations sub-committee of the American Congress in the Spring of 1975, the Arabs could buy up every share on Wall Street within seven months if they so desired, simply by using the surplus profits from oil. Such wealth has its own influence upon the nations seeking economic wellbeing. There is no doubt whatever that this wealth has been used to influence certain nations against Israel. It is now an accepted fact that if the Arabs withdrew their money from London it would spell disaster for Britain. It is now apparent that the Arab intention is to keep up the war atmosphere in order to drain away Israel's life and smash her economy, then when she is at her weakest, the Arabs can deal her a death blow. This plan appears to be working very successfully. With inflation of about twenty-five per cent (it was twenty-three and a half per cent in 1975) recrimination as a result of the war and a good deal of industrial discontent, Israel is facing insolvency. Humanly speaking, her future is bleak. The enormous military resources of her neighbours, the rapidly expanding Arab wealth, Israel's growing isolation, the aloofness (if not coolness) of her former friends, her dwindling foreign exchange and the inevitability of war, all spell Israel's collapse.

There is however, in this dark and gloomy scene one ray of hope which is like the morning star shining in the darkest part of the night to herald the coming of a glorious dawn. It is the Word of God. For Israel is now the cornerstone of world politics, and will be to the end of this age. Through Israel God reveals that history is not a tangle of confused strands, but that in it he is working all things according to the counsel of his will. In Zechariah 12:2, 3, 6, God says, 'I will make Jerusalem and Judah like a cup of poison to all the nearby nations that send their armies to surround Jerusalem. Jerusalem will be a heavy stone burdening the world. And though all the nations of the earth unite in an attempt to move her, they will all be crushed . . . In that day I will make the clans of Judah like a little fire that sets the forest aflame – like a burning match among the sheaves; they will burn up all the neighbouring nations right and left, while Jerusalem stands unmoved' (The Living Bible). That is the one thing we can say, with certainty. Come what may, Jerusalem will be where Jerusalem has ever been, because God has decreed it.

Of course, I deplore the fact that so many lost their lives in the Yom Kippur War, but I thank God that it is one of the means by which he is driving that nation to himself. For I believe that God is bringing the Israelis step by step and stage by stage to realize that they don't have sufficient resources within themselves with which to face the future and that they must therefore look beyond themselves. Their growing isolation among the nations means that they cannot depend on any other nation. The plan of God is in this and something tremendous is happening.

3. Out of Pain, Prayer

Of the one thousand two hundred tanks which Syria threw into the attack on the Golan, only two hundred and forty returned. The Israeli defence forces however, had only seventy tanks on the Golan when the attack came and they fought almost with their bare hands. Most of the men on both fronts were young conscripts, because the rest had been allowed to go home to their families for the Day of Atonement especially those who had been on national service for more than a year or two. So the majority of the soldiers were between eighteen and twenty-one years of age and many were still fasting having had no food or drink for nearly twenty-one hours.

General Rafoul described the way the Israelis held back the Syrians on the Golan Heights in these words: 'We stopped the Syrians by the sheer heroism of soldiers refusing to give way. Each man understood that the choice was either to stand and fight it out, or allow loved ones in the valleys behind them to be slaughtered in the case of a full breakthrough.'

There were many true stories of boys who shot down enemy aeroplanes. The first concerns a Tel Aviv taxi driver, twenty years of age. When one of the MIGs came in low shooting everything up, and everyone else dived for cover, he fired his uzzi, a kind of sten-gun and the plane blew up. After that it became quite a popular pastime to see if one could knock planes out of the sky. The same was true of the tanks. One lad was very badly wounded, so that eventually his foot had to be amputated. The tracks of his tank were damaged, but not the gun. The other crew members were critically wounded, but he was in a position to be able to train the tank gun upon each Syrian tank as it came up over the brow of the hill. Before he was himself put out of action, he knocked out

32

sixteen tanks. We heard many such stories. As the mammoth Syrian attack was checked, many of these stories must have been true.

I remember meeting a boy who was one of only three survivors in a unit of fifty at El Qantarah on the Suez Canal in Northern Sinai. There was another boy who was the only survivor out of two hundred and fifty. In Ein Kerem, a suburb of Jerusalem and the birthplace of John the Baptist, there was scarcely one family that did not suffer bereavement. One of the reasons for this was that it is Israel's policy to send boys from the same area into the same regiment for it is considered good for morale. This means that boys who have grown up together and have gone through school together, go into the same regiment together, which works very well when they do not get killed. However when the fellow with whom you grew up dies alongside you, it is a terrible shock. This too is why in a place like Ein Kerem there was hardly a family unaffected. The whole unit from that area was wiped out.

Israel is unique in that it does not keep its officers in the rear of the battle. They lead their men, following the Old Testament tradition, consequently some of the best young men lose their lives in each of these battles. There is often a tragic aftermath among the survivors too. When most of his unit were either killed or badly wounded, one soldier decided along with two others that the only thing to do was to surrender as they were completely surrounded. They laid out two rows of very badly wounded men, one of sixteen or seventeen and the other of eleven. They put out a white sheet to signal their surrender. It was accepted and the three men were told to stand to one side. When they did this however, the Egyptian tanks moved forward and crushed both lines to death. Twenty-four hours later the boy went out of his mind; his mother, asking for prayer for him, told us, 'He will never be normal again, short of a miracle.'

A taxi cab driver was at a hospital, having taken some friends to visit their wounded son. While there this man saw one of his son's friends, who told him, 'I am very sorry, but your son is dead.' The man decided to go straight home and tell his wife the news. When he got home he found a cable informing them that the elder boy had also been killed. The father then collapsed with a heart attack, and died.

An official in the Foreign Ministry told me about a friend

of his, completely without religious beliefs who came in and said, 'Have you got a prayer hat?' 'Yes,' he replied, 'why?' The friend said, 'I want it. Don't ask me why. I will tell you later.' The official eventually found out that this man's only son had suffered severe brain damage because of shrapnel. The doctor had said that if the boy recovered, he would be a mere cabbage. The father had never prayed before, but he went to his son's bedside and prayed for nine hours that God would take him. After those nine hours, the boy died.

I remember the case of another lad. He had come close to suicide. He was on the Bar-Lev line and was badly shot up. He did not know how many hours he had been unconscious, but when he regained consciousness lying in a pool of his own blood, he realized that he had no legs and thought that he had no arms. So, making a great effort he tried to turn over so that he would roll down into the Suez Canal and drown. As he rolled over, he suddenly realized that he still had one arm attached to his body, although badly wounded. This stopped him and he determined to go on living. That boy was being rehabilitated, along with many other severely wounded men. There are many such stories, but I do not just want to recount harrowing stories for their own sake. It is sufficient to say that there was very very great sadness throughout Israel.

There were other remarkable stories too. There was the Jewish Christian who was called up nineteen times by the military authorities at the wrong address. Finally his whole unit of two hundred and fifty went to the front line without him and there was not a single survivor. Because of an official mix-up, this Jewish Christian survived.

The medical care was amazing. It took on an average only six hours to get a man from the front line to a regular hospital. The new policy of the Israeli Government is to send doctors with their orderlies right into the front lines. You may have seen this on television news reports. Men were shown being brought out with intravenous apparatus already in use. Many of the boys still able to walk, actually walked up to the helicopters holding the intravenous equipment because there was such a scarcity of manpower. I am afraid however, that although many thousands of men were saved by this policy, a number of Israel's finest young doctors lost their lives.

The Hadassah Hospital at Jerusalem performed five hundred and eighty one major operations around the clock in the first twenty days. At their field hospital under canvas, a hundred major operations were performed in this time and these included the most delicate brain surgery. These operations were on men who were too ill to be moved by helicopter into the regular hospitals.

Those in the United States have learned something about burn injuries from the Vietnam War. The Yom Kippur War also had its share. New weapons pierced tank armour-plate and then burst into flames, roasting people alive inside. One must also remember that tanks carry their own ammunition, which explodes when the tank is hit. When I visited the Hadassah Hospital it had a whole top floor given over to men suffering from burns. I was deeply moved by what I saw and heard. The professor taking me around told me, 'Many of these boys are unrecognizable as human beings. They have melted.' Later the professor in charge of the Burns Unit told me that out of sixty or more cases with full-thickness burns (every level of skin tissue being affected), only one died, which is a remarkable tribute to the loving devotion of the doctors and nurses there, who worked day and night to save lives. But most of these men were only eighteen or nineteen years old, with the whole of their lives before them, and those with medical experience will know that such burns cases suffer terrible psychological after-effects.

On a recent visit to the hospital I saw one of these survivors. He had returned there for plastic surgery and further rehabilitation. He was nineteen years of age and must have been a good-looking young man. His face now looked as if it had completely melted — no eyebrows, no eyelashes, hardly any lips and two dark brown eyes looking out from what appeared to be a grotesque mask. Even his hands had melted into grotesque shapes. The professor in charge told me that they had even been able to tell at what time of day the boys had received their burns. At night they were only burnt on their faces and hands, but during the day, especially at midday, the burns were far more extensive because the boys had rolled up their sleeves and opened up their shirts.

We need to pray for these boys, that they might find God. All this affected me so deeply that I told the hospital authorities that my friends and I would make ourselves responsible for the rehabilitation equipment. It has since been my joy to be able to channel over £15,000 of rehabilitation equipment to Hadassah for the use of these boys, some of whom will need care for virtually the rest of their lives.

I have been amazed at the effect that our small gifts have had. On a return visit to Israel, I met all the professors of Hadassah and one after another said, 'We have had some very big gifts, but it was these small gifts from groups of Christian students in Britain and Norway that deeply touched us.' The thing which moved them most of all was that a group in the eastern section of Jerusalem also gave something, for some members of this group were Arab Christians. The Israeli medical authorities remembered that in the 1948 War of Independence, a medical convoy had been ambushed by the Arabs in that very part of the city. Seventy-eight people died in that ambush including the director general of Hadassah, top specialists and doctors, but now after all these years and in a time of need, Arab believers in that same area had joined with other Christians in giving this money.

There were also many cases of paralysis resulting from the Yom Kippur War. There are men who will be lame, dumb or blind for the rest of their lives; there are many others who suffered terrible brain injuries and of course there was much severe shock, as a result of which many cannot speak or see. This was the first war in Israel's twenty-five-year history that resulted in such severe cases of this kind. If there were no other evidence, this would be enough to show the kind of war the Yom Kippur War was. Several of the boys told me that what horrified them most was the fact that the Egyptian troops had been given a drug, something like LSD, which made them completely impervious to fear. Colonel Amnon Resheff, commander of Israel's 14th Armoured Brigade, said, 'Our task was made more difficult by the human waves coming at us. It did not seem to matter how many we killed, they kept on coming. The attacks they made were often suicidal. Their commanders did not care how many perished.'

It is a strange fact but during the whole course of the war I did not personally hear of one Jewish Christian killed or even wounded. I did however, hear of many who had significant opportunities to serve their fellow Israelis on both fronts. One believer from Tel Aviv, named Chaim, was on the Sinai front and had his Bible with him. A big talking point throughout the Israeli army at that time was the question of biblical prophecy, and many were asking, 'Have the Old Testament prophets said anything about the days in which we are living?' Most of these boys knew nothing about the Bible and nothing about prophecy. Whenever they found someone who did, they wanted to hear from him.

Chaim was in great demand everywhere. After the first two weeks of the war, when there was a little more free time, the boys would gather around and discuss these things. They would say, 'Now you read it to us. Where is it?' Then Chaim would lead them in a discussion about the Scriptures. Once a jeep drove up at great speed, and two fellows jumped out of it and ran into the mess hall.

'Where is Chaim? We want Chaim.'

'There are lots of people called Chaim. Which Chaim?' the men in the mess hall answered.

'We want the Bible Chaim.'

'You can't have him, he stays here.'

'We want him down at our end of the Canal, because we have great discussions going on, but no one's got a Bible and no one knows anything about these things.'

At the very height of the war, Arab and Jewish believers were praying together in Jerusalem, but equally remarkable was the fact that those working among the Arabs and those working among the Jews got together. The great breakthrough came after a slight confrontation in one of our times of prayer. First someone prayed for Israel and the Israeli Cabinet. Then someone prayed equally seriously for the Arabs 'for whom our Lord had also died'. I immediately stopped the prayer meeting and said that if we were going to pray horizontally like this and shoot one another down in prayer, we might as well stop altogether. I mentioned that I thought the breakthrough would come when one of those working solely among the Jews, prayed for the Arabs and vice versa.

The change did indeed come when someone who was fanatically pro-Israel prayed that the Arab wounded would really find the Lord and for Arab believers in Damascus that they might be helped by God at that time. That brought us all together and from then on we trusted each other and were able to pray for Arab and Jew alike without recrimination.

The war deeply affected some of the Israeli leaders. Golda Meir, then seventy-six years of age, went to the airport nearly every day on which there were prisoners returning from

Egypt and waited hours to be able to greet them. There were only a few hundred of them in all. At times she wept so much that the television cameras had to be turned away from her. Other times, after a twenty-four hour Cabinet session or something similar, she would go to the hospitals of Hadassah or Tel Hashomer and visit the wounded boys instead of getting some sleep.

The Israeli military authorities often showed humanitarian concern for the welfare of their enemies. I heard about the Syrian pilots who parachuted out of their planes into the sea. Surprisingly it was not the Lebanese government, or the Syrian, but the Israeli authorities who sent launches out to rescue them. I was told of an incident by an Israeli officer when he and his men found the body of a Syrian pilot who had been left unattended within shouting distance of his own units. He had bailed out of his plane and was wounded in his arm and thigh. They were relatively superficial wounds, but he was left to bleed to death when he could easily have been saved by his own troops. On his parachute he had scrawled in Arabic, in his own blood, 'Allah help Syria, if this is the way she treats her sons.'

Most of the Israeli prisoners of war in Egypt were tortured. Some of them will never walk again because of the things which were forced into their bodies. I will not go into the details, but I will however, tell you this. At the Hadassah Hospital one of the leading brain specialists in the world, an Israeli, performed a difficult and complex operation on an Egyptian major and by so doing saved his life. This surgeon's own son will never walk again, because of the way he was tortured by the Egyptians. At the time of his capture he could walk perfectly.

The idea that Israel is an imperialist, colonialist state with a kind of *apartheid* is absolute nonsense. At the Hadassah Hospital, whose standards compare favourably with leading hospitals in London or New York, an assistant surgeon and one of the chief nurses are both Arabs. They work alongside their Jewish colleagues quite happily, which is after all what ideally should happen since Jews and Arabs are cousins. One third of all the out-patients at this hospital are Arab, and about a quarter of the in-patients and there is no distinction made between the two. One cannot help but feel that forces outside the country are playing on this whole matter. If it were not for these outside forces, Arab and Jew would probably live in peace.

I remember speaking with one of the world's leading dermatologists at Hadassah, a specialist in leprosy, who told me 'Just before the war a woman came to us from Cyprus, an Arab woman, and she had the first signs of leprosy. She asked if I could treat her. I said, "Yes, have you any money?" She said, "None at all." So we put her on government expense. During the following months, the fact emerged that her husband was an officer in the Jordanian army, which was facing the Israeli forces. She was totally cured, went back to Jordan and promptly sent a friend to us who also had leprosy, to be cured free of charge at Hadassah.'

There are many signs of a very deep work taking place within the Israeli nation. Golda Meir said in a speech which I found one of the most moving I have ever heard, 'There is no Jew in Israel who can say that he is the same today as he was on the eve of Yom Kippur. I don't believe I will ever be the same.' Bibles and prayer books were in demand above all else by the soldiers and a controversy raged, in the Hebrew press, as to whether the field rabbis (service chaplains) had failed in their duty or not. The crux of the complaint was this – there had been a run on Bibles during the first few weeks of the war, and there were none available.

It was somewhat unreasonable to blame the Jewish chaplaincy. For years no one except perhaps one lad here and there, had ever asked for a Bible. Now suddenly thousands of men wanted them. One Israeli entertainer took a whole truckload of vodka, Bibles and prayer books to the Golan to distribute to the soldiers. It was very cold there, and he took the vodka to try and keep the boys warm. Surprisingly enough, however, it was not the vodka they wanted, but the Bibles which were of course Old Testaments. Some people think that without the New Testament, it is impossible to find God as Saviour and are worried by this, forgetting that the early church had only the Old Testament. The New Testament is of course necessary for the full revelation of God's plan of salvation, but the Old Testament is also the Word of God which lives and abides for ever.

A recent report of interviews with soldiers has revealed that a surprisingly high number of them went into the war as atheists and came out as 'believers'. They are not believers as

Christians understand the word, but believers in a Supreme Being. That is nevertheless a tremendous change of heart. One man told me, 'I have never seen anything like it. The boys prayed before battle, during battle and after battle. They spent time reading the Torah (the first five books of the Bible) and discussing it. I have never seen anything like it. Women normally pray, but not men.'

One great joy was the fact that the Israeli Cabinet officially sanctioned fifteen minutes of Bible reading on the Israeli radio. This had never happened before but now the Bible is read for fifteen minutes during peak listening time each evening.

On November 5th, 1973, a few days before the cease-fire, the chief Rabbi called Israel to prayer. That was the first official day of prayer that the modern state of Israel had ever had and virtually everyone responded to it. The synagogues were packed with people, there were never less than three thousand at the Western Wall in prayer and it was real prayer from the heart. For those of us present on that occasion it was unforgettable. For days afterwards the searing tones of the Rabbi leading us in prayer burnt through our soul. On few occasions can these ancient stones of the Western Wall, spanning as they do the whole age from Christ to the present time and crystallizing the history, sorrow, suffering and hopes of the Jewish people have ever witnessed such prayer.

4. A Searching Nation

There are some evangelical Christians who seem to think that all Israelis are children of God, that angels hover over the street corners of Tel Aviv and that miracles are performed daily throughout Israel. Nothing is farther from the truth. There are probably as many prostitutes in Tel Aviv as there are in Soho, London, or in the slums of any large American city. There are also the usual number of racketeers and swindlers.

Israel by and large is an irreligious nation. Perhaps I ought to explain what I mean by using the adjective 'irreligious' in this connection. There is in Israel a small but vocal and influential religious minority. There is also deep within the Jewish heart a religious awareness. Nevertheless, modern Israel is the product humanly speaking, of early pioneers who were for the most part radical socialists and agnostics. There are a few religious kibbutzim, but for the most part the kibbutzim are irreligious from an orthodox point of view. They observe the festivals and fasts as national holidays rather than for their religious significance. Nearly all the members of the Israeli Cabinet are either atheists or agnostics, excluding of course the National Religious Party member. There are only two others so far as I know, who even vaguely believe in a Supreme Being.

In all the years that I have been travelling to and from Israel and even during the months of the Yom Kippur War, I have never known the Israeli people to be so depressed and despondent as I have found them recently. A pall of depression, almost one of death, hangs over the whole nation. This affects everyone from the young people in the streets to the high officials in the Government. Even people who are normally vivacious and full of humour seem to be under some sort of cloud.

41

I think that this is because Israel feels that she is no longer free to make her own decisions. Her policies are largely being dictated by the Pentagon and other outside forces. She is under pressure to accept conditions which she does not believe are either for her own good or for the good of the Free World. She is trapped in the web of superpower politics.

Added to this is the fact that Israel lost three thousand of her finest young men in the war itself and a further one hundred and eighty died in the ensuing fighting on the Golan. For a nation of only three million people, that is a colossal proportion to have lost. By comparison Syria and Egypt have a combined population of forty-four million people and so are more able to bear their losses. If we were to translate the Israeli figures into British terms, it would mean a loss of sixty-five thousand lives. You can imagine the mourning, sorrow and sense of emptiness which would hang over Britain if she lost that number of young men in a few weeks.

However, the enormous death toll is not the only factor causing this national despondency. There has also been a tremendous amount of inner disunity and recrimination as a result of the war. This actually began during the war itself, when two generals began to argue with one another in public. These were the aggressive and gifted General Ariel Sharon and Major-General Shmuel Gonen, whom many feel was promoted beyond his ability. The quarrel was partly political in origin; most of the other generals are socialists and Sharon belongs to Likud, the liberal-conservative party.

So the whole Israli nation has gone on a kind of orgy of national introspection, investigation and recrimination. Many who have lost sons, husbands, brothers and fathers, have been asking whether the Government did not let them down. This was the first time that Israel had ever been taken by surprise and it is becoming increasingly clear that only a miracle prevented the Arabs from winning the war. Naturally this has shocked the nation, as has the sombre fact that the majority of those who died were in the units that were overrun during the first two days of fighting. There were hardly any survivors from these units. Those bereaved are charging the Government with criminal negligence. They may not necessarily have the truth on their side, but this is their charge.

As a result of all this, David Elazar resigned and Mordechai Gur, another general, took his place as

Commander-in-Chief. This may be good for the country. Incidentally, Mordechai Gur is the writer of the most popular children's fairy stories in Israel. There can be few who combine such qualities. Moshe Dayan, also stepped down, and I am sure that this will be to Israel's loss. Golda Meir finally resigned because at her age she eventually found the inner disharmony, backbiting and bickering in her coalition of left-wing parties too much of a strain. It was sad to see someone who had served her people so valiantly and sacrificially, leave office in these circumstances. She has stated that she will not be able to forgive herself that she did not follow her intuition on that Friday (October 5th, 1973) and call for a general mobilization. Instead she trusted her military advisers. Whatever mistakes may have been made, Golda Meir is one of the truly great personalities of this generation. So Yitzhak Rabin, who was something of an unknown quantity when he took office, became Prime Minister. Previously he had been an army general and a very successful ambassador to the United States. He is a highly intelligent and capable man and is proving to be a strong and resilient leader.

Probably the biggest shock that Israel received was at the end of May 1974, when it became public knowledge that the United States had concluded an agreement with Egypt the previous January to give her a nuclear reactor. At no time had Kissinger acquainted any member of the Israeli Cabinet with this decision. Nixon, Kissinger and Joseph Sisco, a long-time United States negotiator in the Middle East, have all said on a number of occasions that American policy towards Israel has not changed. This is just not true. It has undergone a colossal change, not so much in America's dealings with Israel, as in her dealings with Israel's neighbours. She is seeking to bring Egypt, Jordan, and Syria into her orbit of influence and so cannot give Israel the same kind of support as previously. Obviously the development and maintenance of friendly relations with these Arab nations must have an effect on America's attitude to Israel herself.

I believe that all this has something to do with Israel's present spiritual condition. She is beginning to feel totally isolated, even from her one staunch and faithful friend, the United States. The United States has rearmed Israel and will continue to rearm Israel, but the Common Market nations are not going to help her and neither are the nations of the Third World. The United States is her only friend and therefore has the upper hand. She pays the piper and she can call the tune. Israel knows full well that Kissinger has only to withhold her desperately needed economic aid, or to refuse to sell her the latest weapons and that would be the end.

In addition to this is a sense of hopelessness and despondency that the last war, which should have finished up with Damascus and Cairo at Israel's mercy, instead saw the whole Israeli triumph taken away from her by American intervention and pressure. Israel now feels that in winning, she did not win. In fact, she was robbed of a first-rate victory that could have shattered the invading armies and rendered them inoperative for at least five years. With hostile armies not only intact but rearmed, with no added security (in fact, far less), and with so many dead, her people quite naturally are asking, 'Was it all worth it?'

When we gather all these strands together, we can begin to understand the despondency which has settled upon the Israeli people. The nation's growing isolation, the inevitability of renewed war, the spectre of insolvency and economic ruin, the inner disharmony and recrimination resulting from the war, the enormous resources of wealth in the Arab nations arrayed against her, the Soviet Union's undisguised hatred and the likelihood of her coming into the next round of fighting – all of this more than explains the despondency and depression.

What then is the spiritual condition of Irael now? I do not believe that great military triumphs on their own would ever bring the Jewish people to Christ. These only foster their sense of self-assurance. We can well understand such self-assurance, for it has been produced by the tough, pioneering spirit which owes no man anything. It was this indpendent self-sufficiency which turned arid deserts and malarial swamplands into fields and gardens. The Arabs did not want such malarial swamps or barren wastes and sold them for high prices. They were bought by the early settlers. Basically no one supported them. A large number of them died in the process, but others carried on until finally the orchards, vineyards and farms of modern Israel took shape. Israel has had to fight the whole way not only in the early days but in every successive phase she has had to contend for her very existence. This spirit of proud independence and self-sufficiency has resulted in a certain amount of arrogance and cockiness. The miliary triumphs of the last twenty-five years moreover, have only increased this. It is the kind of spirit that said, 'You only have to fire a few shots in the air and the Syrians run like rabbits. You only have to point a tank in the direction of Cairo and the Egyptians collapse immediately.' All that has now disappeared. Israel has lost her arrogance and the Yom Kippur War is the reason. That war and its aftermath have made Israelis realize that they need some kind of moral strength and power which they do not have in themselves. The fact that their one great friend, the United States, appears to be withdrawing and taking up a new and more impartial position, means that the Israelis feel somewhat bereft and insecure. I believe that for the first time Israel is beginning to feel her need for some kind of power beyond herself. She has not lost her courage or her will to fight, but she has started on an inner quest. That quest will end in a discovery of the living God.

When I visited Christian friends in Jerusalem recently, they told me that they had never before had so many enquiries from young Jewish people as at present. The attitude of Jewish Russian immigrants is an encouragement too, since some of them are Christians. In the Soviet Union everyone grows up in an atheist environment and the Jews have been as much oppressed as Gentiles in religious matters. The Russians officially respect their background but it is as much frowned upon to go to synagogue as it is to go to chapel or church and everyone has to listen to endless discussions about the worthlessness of religion. In spite of this some have found the Messiah. Since they are very conscious of being Jewish they have applied for visas to come to Israel as Jews.

The many complex and insoluble problems confronting the Israeli people at the present time are undoubtedly being used by God to force her into a new position. The Lord is cornering Israel. Step by step and stage by stage, God is shutting up Israel to himself. In the end there will be no way out except through him. Israelis are beginning to look at their own history to rediscover the inner significance of their survival. I believe that this is the first sign of the Holy Spirit's new working among the Jewish people.

5. Gog and Magog?

27/6/83

During the Yom Kippur War all Israel was talking about
Gog and Magog. There are two old Jewish gentlemen, who
have at different times written independent articles on the
biblical prophets with particular regard to the numbers given
by them. Using rabbinic methods these men came up with a
series of past and future dates important to Israel. The dates
are: 1880, 1917, 1948, 1967, 1973–74.

Their findings would by no means meet with the approval
of the majority of Bible scholars and should be evaluated
with very real caution. Although both these men were
interviewed at various times on Israeli television and radio
and articles appeared about their findings in newspapers and
magazines, they were never taken seriously. They were
regarded as lovable eccentrics. They published the results of
their work in books and pamphlets in Hebrew, the latest in
1968.

Of course 1880 was a remarkable date in the history of
Israel because it marked the first great wave of immigrants
(especially Ukrainian and Russian–Polish) out of which a
whole number of settlements and cities arose, for example,
Rishon le-Zion, Petah Tikvah, Degania and Rosh Pinna.
1917 saw the Balfour Declaration of a Jewish homeland. In
that document Arthur James Balfour, the British Foreign
Secretary, declared that 'His Majesty's Government views
with favour the establishment of a national home for the
Jewish people, and will use their best endeavours to facilitate
the achievement of this object.' In 1948 there was the re-
creation of the State of Israel against overwhelming odds.
1967 marked the return of Jerusalem to Jewish administration and control for the first time in two thousand years,
with the exception of a few months in A.D. 135. Both of these

old gentlemen agreed in principle upon 1973–74 as the year when the war of Gog and Magog was to occur.

I must say that in all the years that I have been travelling to Israel and I am generally there for at least four months each year, I have never known Israel more relaxed or peaceful than in August and September 1973, just before the war. One could drive along any of her borders without problem. At one point I nearly drove over into Lebanon by mistake.

Suddenly, on the Day of Atonement of all days and without warning, the worst and most severe of Israel's four wars began with a massive attack on two fronts. The Israeli people began to talk. Many of them said, 'Do you remember that old man who was interviewed on television? Didn't he say something about 1973–74?' Others remembered what the newspapers and magazines had printed about the two men's findings. Everywhere people began to talk about Gog and Magog.

Soldiers on both fronts were asking whether the Hebrew prophets had said anything about the present conflict or what was to follow it. Teachers told me that even children came up to them and asked, 'Would you please tell me about Gog and Magog? What is it?' As Christian teachers are not allowed to influence minors in religious matters, one teacher when asked that question by a child, sent him home to ask his parents. The following day the little boy came back and said, 'My parents say they want to know what Gog and Magog means too.'

There are few subjects on which such widely differing views have been held than on the subject of Gog and Magog. Much controversy has been generated by it, and it would be well for us to exercise extreme caution as we approach such a matter. For instance, we should, I think, be careful about these dates, as we should also be about some of the more extreme interpretations of chapters 38 and 39 of the book of Ezekiel. Personally I feel that great damage has been done by those prophetic systems that spell out all the details, and that to give such a dogmatic and detailed sequence of events is dangerous. There is nothing wrong with a personal view, provided it is open to correction and further revelation. On the other hand the greatest tragedy of all is when we make our view of prophecy the ground for faction, division and wild and extreme actions.

So often these matters are revealed to us as they happen. For instance, Jerusalem was taken by Israel in 1967. At that time I said publicly in a number of places, 'Now we must wait and see. If in a year's time Jerusalem is still under Jewish control, we will know that the prophecy of our Lord in the Gospel of Luke has been fulfilled.' That was in 1967. Jerusalem has not only remained in Jewish hands, it has been unified under an Israeli administration. I think that that event has given us a very real key to a number of other prophecies. The same was true of the re-creation of the state of Israel in 1948.

We can especially learn about the Gog–Magog prophecy from Ezekiel 38 and 39. Chapter 38 mentions a number of names – Gog of the land of Magog, prince of Rosh, Meshech and Tubal (vv. 2–3), Persia, Cush, and Put (v.5), Gomer and Togarmah (v.6), Sheba, Dedan, and Tarshish (v.13). It is interesting to find a number of these names linked together in Genesis 10:2–4. Gog could be a person or a people. Magog in Hebrew is literally 'of Gog' or 'from Gog'. It is probably the name of a place derived from Gog. It would appear that originally Gog and Magog were associated with Asia Minor. The prince of Rosh could as easily be translated 'the chief prince of Meschech and Tubal'. Rosh in Hebrew means 'chief' or 'head', and is so translated in the Authorized version and other translations of the Bible. Some would identify Rosh with Rash, a place west of Elam, modern Iran. It is interesting that in Hebrew the letter *aleph* is used, although we now pronounce the word 'rosh'. This could point to 'rash' being the original pronunciation.

Meshech and Tubal are found linked together throughout Scripture. See Genesis 10:2, and Ezekiel 27:13; 32:26. Both were located east of Asia Minor. Persia presents no real difficulty, although it covered a larger territory than modern Iran. Cush is normally understood as Ethiopia, but was more centred on modern Sudan than modern Ethiopia. Put is often identified as Libya, as in the Authorized version of the Bible. This identification is possible, but it is more probably modern Somalia and Eritrea in East Africa. Gomer is to be located north of the Black Sea, Togarmah in Armenia, and Sheba and Dedan in modern Saudi Arabia, south and north respectively. Merchants of Tarshish were Phoenicians originating in Tyre and Sidon, modern Lebanon. All these names, excluding the last three, are seen as actually involved in the planned invasion of Israel. Sheba, Dedan and the merchants of Tarshish stand to gain much as less involved collaborators.

There have been widely differing views as to the identification of these names with modern nations. For example, there is the widely held view that Rosh is to be identified with Russia, Meshech with Moscow, Tubal with Tobolsk, and Gomer with Germany or Eastern Europe. While this view cannot be reliably supported, we must note that three times it is stated that the invading forces will come from 'the uttermost parts of the north' (Ezekiel 38:6, 15; 39:2). Moreover in Ezekiel 38:6 it is Togarmah that is mentioned in connection with the uttermost parts of north, but in 38:15 and 39:2 it is Gog. It is worth noting that the modern versions of the Bible rightly translate this as the 'uttermost parts' (Revised standard version of the Bible) 'the remote parts' (New American Standard Bible), and 'the far recesses' (New English Bible), and that the Authorized version ('north quarters', 'north parts') is not accurate here. It is not good enough to say that this phrase meant the northern fringe of the known world at that time, that is Armenia and cannot mean anything beyond the Caucasus. The prophecy was given for the understanding of those living in the last times and to them the uttermost north must mean just that. Thus while we should be careful about identifying these names with Moscow, Tobolsk, Germany, etc., the uttermost parts of north, in relation to Israel can mean only the Soviet Union.

Another small but interesting point is that the name Ashkenazi (see Genesis 10:2–4) is the name given in modern Jewry, through long usage, to all Jews originating in northern and central Europe speaking Yiddish, that is those from Russia, the Ukraine, Poland, Germany, etc. All Jews originating in the south, that is Oriental and Latin Jews, are called Sephardim.

A far more important point is that nearly all the invasions in Israel's history have been from the north or from the south, and hardly any from the west or the east. These invading nations may not have been geographically situated in the north, but in the east, such as Babylon and Persia. In the war described by Ezekiel the nations may likewise come from many quarters, but they will invade from the north and it is there that this whole confederacy of evil will be militarily centred.

What then can we conclude from this? We can say with some certainty that Ezekiel, by the Spirit of God, used these names to symbolize powers north, south, east, and west of Israel, nations hostile to the purpose of God. He appears to predict a gathering of these nations led and armed by certain northern powers. He also implies if he does not actually state, that the invasion will be from the north. (See Ezekiel 38:15; cf. v.9.) Gog and Magog appear in early Jewish literature after Ezekiel's time as symbolizing in general the leaders of world powers hostile to God and his purpose. Many Jewish sources since have regarded Gog and Magog as describing northern barbaric nations. As early as the first century after Christ, Josephus, the Jewish general and historian (c. A.D. 37–100), identified them with the Scythians. These were themselves a nomadic tribe originating in western Siberia and living between the Black and Caspian Seas. In general usage the name 'Scythians' came to describe any number of northern barbaric tribes controlling the steppe lands and trade routes of Russia. Many identify the Scythians with the Ashkenaz.

There are widely differing views as to whether we have any clear indication as to when all this is to take place. Very much depends upon whether one believes that the reference to Gog and Magog in Revelation 20:8 is to the same war as in Ezekiel 38 and 39. If one believes that it is and that there is to be a Millennium, then it must come at the end of the Millennium. There are, however, real difficulties here. Ezekiel 38 and 39 refer to an Israel which has been regathered and re-created as a nation. Yet there is no mention of the Messiah as present in their midst and we are told that the Holy Spirit will be poured out upon them after this war. (See Ezekiel 39:29.) Furthermore it would appear that the war takes place after the re-creation of the state of Israel, but before all Jews have been regathered. (See Ezekiel 38:8; cf. 39:28.) None of this fits the usual Millennial view.

A number hold the view that the battle of Armageddon (Revelation 16:14–16.) is to be equated with the Gog and Magog war of Ezekiel 38 and 39. Just because contending nations meet together in battle in the Middle East does not mean Armageddon is upon us, not even if the point of contention is Israel herself. Undoubtedly there will be a number of serious battles over Israel involving many nations.

They will not necessarily be Armageddon. In one sense there may well be a number of 'mini-Armageddons'. We have several examples of this principle in Scripture. For instance the words of our Lord about the destruction of Jerusalem (Matthew 24, Luke 21, Mark 13) were not exhaustively fulfilled in the city's destruction in A.D. 70, but appear to await a further and final fulfilment.

We have further examples of this in the Old Testament prophecies which had their first fulfilment in the return from Babylon and yet were not exhaustively fulfilled then. Perhaps this principle is most clearly seen in the matter of the Antichrist. Daniel's prophecies concerning him were first fulfilled in Antiochus IV Epiphanes (c. 163 B.C.) and so Antiochus became the archetype of Antichrist in Scripture. Down through the years believers have seen the Antichrist in a number of historic personalities. For example, Nero, Napoleon, Hitler, Mussolini, Stalin. All these men were 'mini-Antichrists' in so far as the spirit of Antichrist was in them. They were all to a greater or lesser degree demon-inspired. The final Antichrist will sum them all up, entirely eclipsing them.

In the same way it could be that we shall have several 'mini-Armageddons', when the nations of the world collide over Israel. In my estimation the war in Ezekiel 38 and 39 could well be the most serious of these.

It is relevant to ask whether the reference in Ezekiel 38:11 to 'unwalled villages' gives any indication of time? Many would say that Israel is like a fortress at present. Can we say that Israel is 'at rest' or 'dwelling securely' (v.11)? This is a more serious objection. In the whole twenty-eight years of modern Israel's history she could hardly ever have been termed 'at rest'. On the other hand, one has only to speak to older Israelis, who have known the pogroms,* the Nazi era and the ghettos, to hear them say that the present era in fact spells comparative security and freedom for them. It is also only in the last century that there have been unwalled cities, towns and villages in Israel.

One thing is very clear from Scripture; at the very point when it seems that Israel will be destroyed, there will be an intervention from heaven and the whole of the military confederation from the north will go up in smoke. Israel will

*See Appendix.

spend seven months burying the dead. That confederacy, having planned finally to solve the Israeli problem by annihilating her completely, will itself be wiped out. Whether the miraculous intervention of God will be a divinely-timed earthquake or something nuclear, we do not know. It is a real possibility that as has happened so many times in the history of the people of God, the enemy's own weapons will backfire on him. The very means by which he has planned to destroy Israel could come back on him; a ballistic missile for instance, could fall short and destroy the whole northern confederacy. What we do know is that they will be destroyed by divine intervention, in a single moment of time.

God has said that he is not only going to send fire on Magog, but also on 'those who dwell securely in the coastlands' (Ezekiel 39:6 Revised Standard version). In the Authorized version the word 'coastlands' is translated 'isles'. The Hebrew word was originally used to describe the islands of Greece, but came to mean all that lies beyond Israel to the west. Surely this indicates that in some way the Western World will be involved in this 'blowup' in the Middle East. It would be well for all those who dwell so securely in the West to ponder on these words. So many of the free Western nations are ripe for judgment.

Let's summarize the points upon which there is some certainty:

1. This planned invasion of Israel is at the time of the end, the last part of the age. (Ezekiel 38:8, 'latter years', literally 'end of years'; Ezekiel 38:16, 'latter days'.)

2. Israel is again dwelling in the land, i.e. Israel is re-created as a state. (Ezekiel 38:8, 14.)

3. There is a gathering of nations against Israel from all sides – north and south, east and west – but the attack is from the north. (Ezekiel 38:1 1–6 13; 39:2.)

4. The phrase 'uttermost parts of the north' is mentioned three times. (Ezekiel 38:6, 15; 39:2.) There must be some significance in our attention being drawn not just to the north but to the uttermost parts of the north.

5. Reference is made to the fact that these nations will be armed to a quite exceptional degree. (Ezekiel 38:4; 39:9, 10.)

6. The destruction of this great armed confederacy is by divine intervention. (Ezekiel 38:18–22; 39:3–10.)

7. The destruction takes place upon the mountains of

Israel and is colossal and final. It will be the end of the northern powers. (Ezekiel 39:2–20.)

8. It would appear that more than the Middle East is to be affected by this war and God's intervention in it. (Ezekiel 39:6. Note 'the coastlands' or 'the isles'.)

9. It will result in the final ingathering of the Jewish people to Israel. (Ezekiel 39:21–28.)

10. The Holy Spirit will be poured out upon them after the war. (Ezekiel 39:29.)

In my view the stage is now being set for a military catastrophe over Israel which will be of real consequence to the rest of the world. Whether this will be the Gog and Magog war of Ezekiel 38 and 39 or not is open to question. As I have already stated, there are many interesting features developing in the present Middle East situation which could link it with Ezekiel 38 and 39, but it would be foolish to be dogmatic over this. The next war though serious, may only be part of the buildup. Whether the Gog and Magog war described by Ezekiel comes within the next year or the next decade, it will surely come and it could all happen in a moment.

6. Will Israel Survive?

'The conflict in the Holy Land was the beginning of a war we all lost.' So stated London's *Sunday Telegraph* concerning the Yom Kippur War. One thing is certain – the Yom Kippur War was not the end but another chapter in a continuing drama.

Israel has survived the most powerful onslaught yet made upon her and I believe we have grounds for believing that she will survive every further onslaught. The Lord God has given us his word on this matter in Amos, chapter 9:14, 15: 'I will restore the captivity of my people Israel and they will rebuild the ruined cities and live in them, they will also plant vineyards and drink their wine, and make gardens and eat their fruit. I will also plant them on their land, and they will not again be rooted out from their land which I have given them' (New American Standard Bible). Again this thought is enlarged upon in Zechariah, ' "I will make Jerusalem and Judah like a cup of poison to all the nearby nations that send their armies to surround Jerusalem. Jerusalem will be a heavy stone burdening the world. And though all the nations unite in an attempt to move her, they will all be crushed. In that day," says the Lord, "I will bewilder the armies drawn up against her and make fools of them, for I will watch over the people of Judah, but blind all her enemies . . . In that day I will make the clans of Judah like a little fire that sets the forest aflame – like a burning match among the sheaves; they will burn up all the neighbouring nations right and left, while Jerusalem stands unmoved . . . For my plan is to destroy all the nations that come against Jerusalem" ' (Zechariah 12:2–4, 6, 9, The Living Bible).

'Jerusalem will be a heavy stone burdening the world.' This statement has a remarkably contemporary ring about it. For in fact the Yom Kippur War was only another phase in the battle for Jerusalem. It is clear that war will be renewed, regardless of whether there will be a period of disengagement or of some agreement on minor issues. Indeed, in all probability Israel is now facing the most terrible conflict in all of her twenty-eight-year history. Who would have thought even thirty years ago that the Jewish people, with a third of their number liquidated in the concentration camps of Nazi occupied Europe would again be a nation amongst the nations of the world? Who would have thought that Jerusalem would be a bone of contention among the nations of the world, and that Israel would be the focal point of strife and war? Who would have thought that this little nation, then not even in existence as a sovereign state, would be the spark to set off a third world conflagration? Who could have foreseen, humanly speaking, that Jerusalem would again become the capital of this dispersed and frequently persecuted people?

It is interesting that the late King Faisal of Saudi Arabia said again and again that Jerusalem was the real point of contention, not the Golan or the Sinai or the West Bank. The Rabat Conference of Arab nations in 1974 endorsed this view by putting Jerusalem at the heart of the conflict. Now Israel may be prepared to give up Sinai, much of the West Bank, and perhaps even more of the Golan, but without doubt Israel will never surrender Jerusalem. We can therefore see that in the last phase of world history, Jerusalem will indeed be a heavy stone burdening the whole world.

The prospects facing Israel now are very simple. She is confronted by two stark alternatives – either she withdraws or she does not. All the Arab nations have made it abundantly clear that renewal of the conflict is the only possibility if Israel does not give up all the land occupied in 1967; so if Israel does not withdraw there will be war. Israel has indicated that she would be prepared to give up much of the Sinai, and has already returned the Abu Rhodeis oilfield and certain strategic passes. She would also consider surrendering most of the West Bank. She has however already returned nearly all she can in the Golan and to give back more would be to lay the whole of upper Galilee at the mercy of enemy attack.

The fact that the Rabat Conference recognized the Palestinian Liberation Organization as the only representa-tive of the Palestinian people, thus excluding King Hussein and Jordan, has complicated the issue considerably. This is why King Hussein has had to adopt a decisively more warlike attitude towards Israel. He believes this to be the only way that he can regain prestige and position in the Arab world and be recognized, at the least, as a representative of the Palestinian people. I do not think that Israel would be prepared to give back the West Bank to the P.L.O., allowing it to become a hostile Marxist-orientated state situated right at her heart.

In recent months Yasser Arafat, the leader of the P.L.O. has been putting forward apparently more moderate proposals. He has not spoken as previously about 'driving the Jews into the sea' but has declared repeatedly that the aim of the P.L.O. is to replace the 'racist state of Israel' by a 'democratic secular state of Palestine'. This would be a state he asserts, in which 'Muslims, Christians and Jews would live together as citizens with equal rights under the rule of law as in the Lebanon'. The events in the Lebanon during 1975 must surely give the lie to that.

It must however be understood that one of the strongest grounds for the existence of a Jewish state has been that Jews should no longer be a minority in the midst of a non-Jewish majority. Golda Meir has stated that she would rather emigrate to France or Britain and be part of the Jewish minority there than be in a Jewish minority in a 'democratic secular state of Palestine'. The history of the past two thousand years furnishes us with continuous evidence of the unjust discrimination and persecution of Jewish minorities. Yasser Arafat's proposed secular state of Palestine does not give any guarantees in practice that history will not repeat itself. The leopard has not changed its spots. It is surely out of the question in the light of history to expect the Jewish people to surrender their sovereignty so hardly won and to give their destiny into the 'kind' hands of a non-Jewish majority.

I am continually amazed at the dimensions of the conflict which rages over this small state consisting of three million people and covering less than eight thousand square miles. It seems to be neither logical nor reasonable. What do the Arabs with their hundreds of thousands of square miles desire so greatly in those few square miles of Israel? There are no great natural resources of oil, natural gas or coal such as is found in Arab territories. Apart from some valuable chemicals found in the Dead Sea region there are few commercial reasons to desire Israel. Israel does not possess great rivers such as are found in Syria, Iraq and Egypt, the Euphrates and the Nile, which once harnessed could make the desert blossom as the rose and provide plenty of fertile land to support their populations. Israel has only the river Jordan, a river not as big as the river Thames, which she has not been slow to harness, but which cannot be compared with the tremendous potentialities of the Euphrates or the Nile.

The heart of the problem is the Palestinian refugee. We are told constantly that the cause of the whole conflict is the plight of the Palestinians. Israel insists that about six hundred thousand of these folk fled in 1948 at the instigation of Arab broadcasts from Damascus, Amman and Cairo. They were told to leave in order to allow the Arab armies a free and unhindered hand in the conquest of Israel and that they would return within weeks in the wake of the Arab triumph. Arab sources put the figure of refugees much higher, about nine hundred thousand, and assert that they were all expelled by force. How then is it that there are Arab-Israeli citizens? The answer is that they are the Arabs who did not flee. I have no doubt that as always in times of war and strife, the good is not all on one side. There were blots on the Israeli record but far from it being the Israeli policy to expel the Arabs, loudspeaker vans toured Arab areas pleading with them to stay.

The sad fact is that the Palestinian refugee has become a pawn in a political game. The Arab wealth from increased oil revenue in the past few years alone, could have settled every Palestinian refugee in their own homestead with a livelihood, but it has been Western money that has paid for the welfare of Arab refugees. Basically it has not suited the Arab nations to absorb the Palestinian refugee but to keep them herded in camps in order to prompt world opinion against Israel. Thus the plight of the Palestinian is indeed sad. They are among the most attractive, and industrious of the Arab peoples, but unwanted by all. It is the more sad when it is realized that this problem could have been settled years ago.

It is also interesting that the world never hears about the Jewish refugees from Arab lands. During 1948, at the same time as the Palestinian refugee problem began, many thousands of Jews were expelled from Arab countries, their

property was confiscated and their bank balances frozen and
then taken over. They were expelled with only the clothes they
stood up in. Their plight has never been debated in the United
Nations nor has it ever become the basis for any U.N.
resolutions. None of them have ever received any indemnity
for what they have lost. Furthermore, they were never kept in
refugee camps in Israel but absorbed, settled and rehabilitated by the Jewish Agency. The refugee problem is not all
one-sided. It might be well to underline here that the
treatment of Jewish minorities in Arab lands does not give rise
to any confidence in Yasser Arafat's dream of a democratic
state of Palestine.

In the end it is Jerusalem that will be the real bone of
contention, rather than any of these other areas, for if Israel
is not prepared to give up Jerusalem, there is bound to be a
resumption of war. I have found that most Israelis would be
prepared to give up the major part of the territory occupied in
the 1967 war provided that in return they could receive
guaranteed and secure boundaries and genuine peace.
Jerusalem however, they will not give up. Jerusalem has
hardly ever been without a Jewish population during the past
two thousand years and at many times this has been in the
majority. During the latter part of the 19th century the Jews
accounted for two thirds of the city's population and since
this time they have remained in the majority. To the Jewish
heart there is no alternative to Jerusalem and it is unthinkable
for them to give it up. To the Muslim however it ranks but
third or fourth in the holy places in Islam. Whereas, for
example, every Mosque throughout the world is built in such a
way that for prayer all face towards Mecca, not Jerusalem, in
Jewish liturgy, thought and prayer, Jerusalem is central.
There is no alternative to Jerusalem for the Jewish people.

Israel may well be forced to withdraw substantially. The
United States has been exerting maximum pressure on her to
do so and since Israel depends upon the United States for
most of the economic and military aid that she needs, this
pressure is very telling. Golda Meir has said that many in the
West think Israel only wants to grab land, but Israel only
wants what she has farmed for many years. If Israel
withdraws, a third world war is inevitable, because America
would have to guarantee Israel's frontiers and the Soviet
Union those of Syria and Egypt. For the first time the stage

would be set for a direct superpower confrontation and collision would be inevitable.

In early summer 1974, Israel's Prime Minister, Yitzhak Rabin, broadcast to the Israeli people, warning them that war might well resume within a year and that they must be ready and braced for the next assault. Obviously no Prime Minister would make such a statement without reliable information. His broadcast was in fact based on information collected by Israeli intelligence forces. I mentioned earlier the tremendous military buildup in the Arab nations, particularly in Syria and Iraq. While Egypt has so far had difficulty in persuading the Soviet Union to replace the weapons lost in the last war and is not up to her former military strength, Syria has trebled hers, and indeed is now one vast arsenal.

According to Israeli Intelligence the Soviet Union has supplied Syria with the latest MIG 23 fighter, previously found only in the East German and Soviet air forces, and has also been supplying Syria with the latest Soviet weapons which were not found in her armoury during the Yom Kippur War. For the first time Israeli Intelligence has reported to the United Nations that Soviet officers and men are openly manning missile batteries in Syria. So Syria's repeated claim that she now has long-range missiles which could hit every city and settlement within Israel is not an empty one.

Since the disengagement on the Golan in May 1974, Syria has been quite outspoken in her newspaper articles and editorials (nearly all of which are government-controlled) saying that war will be resumed. The very demands she is making upon Israel, she knows Israel cannot possibly fulfil.

Iraq has also been receiving weapons from the Soviet Union in unprecedented numbers. She now has one thousand Soviet T54 and T62 tanks. She has also received various missiles, including Scud ground-to-ground missiles. She has been supplied with three hundred and fifty planes by the Soviet Union, including the new Tupolev 22 long-range bomber. The Tupolev 22 had previously not been given to any other air force than that of the Soviet Union herself. In addition there are now more than a thousand Soviet advisers in the Iraqi armed forces. On top of all this is the Soviet naval build-up in the Indian Ocean, Red Sea, and Mediterranean. There are a remarkable number of Soviet personnel in strategic positions at the entrance to the Red Sea.

Every Syrian and Egyptian soldier captured in the last war was equipped with gear for radioactive fallout and biological bacterial warfare. None of the Israeli defence forces were equipped in this way. One cannot help drawing the conclusion that it was expected that nuclear and bacterio-logical weapons would be used at some time during the course of the war, and on my information, the Soviet Union very nearly permitted this.

We must take note too of the warning given by Israel's President Katzir in 1974, when he said that Israel had the capacity to produce nuclear warheads and was working hard on the project. He also gave a solemn warning to all the nations of the world by saying that Israel would not hesitate to use them if she had to. It is also a widely held view that Israel has an A-bomb, and if this is so, and there is no reason at all to doubt it, if Israel had her back against the wall, she would undoubtedly use it. Recent reports estimate that Israel has some twenty nuclear devices, a larger number than generally believed.

From all this emerge some interesting facts. It appears that the real threat of renewed war is now from the north rather than from the south. A regrouping has taken place consisting of Syria, Jordan, Iraq, and the P.L.O., heavily backed by the Soviet Union, and this now constitutes the real threat. Egypt on the other hand, appears to be open to some kind of negotiated settlement. Referring back to the war predicted in Ezekiel 38 and 39, it is interesting to note that Egypt is not mentioned in the array of nations against Israel. If this regrouping becomes a substantial feature, we have the first possible sign that the time of its fulfilment is upon us. In the alliance of nations mentioned there, Iran is now the only nation which has not set herself against Israel. Ethiopia and the Sudan (Cush), Libya or Somalia and Eritrea (Put), along with Saudi Arabia (Dedan and Sheba) are all now involved in some way.

In a renewal of war in the Middle East, would the fighting be contained in that area, or would it spread to the whole world? At the time many thought of the Yom Kippur War as a merely Middle East affair, a localized Israeli conflict, but we can now see that it had grave significance for the whole world. There is not a nation in the Free World that is not suffering from its economic consequences and we shall see in the future that very much more began with that war. The Arab oil producers have already stated that in any renewal of the conflict, there would be a total embargo on oil supplies for the duration of hostilities which alone would be enough to send many national economies over the edge of economic ruin. Thus the outlook for the Free World is dark even if the war does not spread beyond the Middle East.

This is why the United States has had to declare openly that in the event of a total Arab oil embargo, she could not rule out the possibility of a military takeover of the Arab oil fields. I cannot help feeling that if the United States were to intervene on Israel's side using military force, Russia could well move at lightning speed and occupy Europe. There could then be an exchange of nuclear weapons between the United States and Russia which would leave very much on both sides of the Atlantic devastated.

U.S. servicemen stationed in Germany, certainly those in Intelligence whom I have spoken to, say that the Warsaw Pact countries (i.e. the U.S.S.R. and her satellites) could easily sweep over Western Europe, and that NATO forces could not hold out in Germany for more than a day or two. The Warsaw Pact countries have colossal numerical strength; for example Poland alone has six hundred fighter bombers. Of course, we do not know how loyal many of these Eastern European forces would be in such a war.

Soviet tactics and strategy can however, be seen clearly in the way they treated Czechoslovakia. They did not only start at the borders, but they dropped parachute regiments on the airport in Prague and took it within an hour. Then the great air transports came in one after another, carrying tanks and everything else right into the heart of the country. This is why one top NATO expert with long and wide experience has said that the Soviet Union and her allies could occupy the Western capitals in four hours by simply seizing their airports, for once you have the airports, you have the countries right at their hearts.

It is a sad fact that we do not now have even one strong government in the Free World. Indeed at the time of writing, Italy, France, Germany, Holland, Belgium, Denmark, Sweden, Norway and Britain all have minority governments. Portugal's previous strong government, whatever we may have felt about its politics, has now been replaced by a new one which appears to be very shaky. One feels that a similar crisis could occur in Spain at any time. Even in Italy there is a growing communist influence that may well take over. At no point in its history has NATO been in such disarray and in such a state of weakness. Owing to inflation one Western Government after another has been cutting its defence costs, the most notable being Britain. The whole of Europe is in a weak state and this is reflected in the absence of great statesmen. Even in the United States, there does not seem to be the overall confidence of the people in the Presidency as previously.

The Soviet Union has said for years that the Free World would drop into their hands like over-ripe fruit when the time came and fourteen years ago she planned to take Free Europe via Israel, Arab oil and North Africa. There can have been few times since the end of the Second World War when the Free World has been in such disarray economically, financially and politically as it is today; much of the Free World is at present engrossed in its own domestic crises and is militarily weak and unprepared. The civil and military leaders of the Soviet Union must be sorely tempted to take advantage of the present situation. It could well be that a further conflict in the Middle East will provide them with the excuse they need.

It is a fact that the Soviet Union has never ceased in the past few years to build up her forces. She has now reached proportions of incredible strength. Apart from certain tactical weapons she has superior strength in nearly every field. It is both naïve and childish to believe that this military build-up is merely for defence. Nuclear submarines are not defensive weapons and these are being produced at the rate of one a month. We are drawn to the conclusion that Russia is bent on world domination. 'Détente' has been and is being used by them to this end. There is no ocean where the Russian Navy is not found and we must face the solemn fact that all the shipping lanes could be cut by them at will. A number of world leaders have drawn attention recently to this threat. Mrs Margaret Thatcher, the leader of the Conservative party has been quite outspoken when commenting on the Russian military build-up. James Schlesinger, at one time Defence Secretary of the United States has repeatedly warned world opinion about the dangers of the Kissinger 'détente' policy.

Recently he likened the Soviet military build-up to that of the Nazis in the 1930s, but hastened to point out that the world took more notice of the Nazis, because of their bombast than of the quiet Soviet attitude. Alexander Solzhenitsyn that great champion of truth has fearlessly and repeatedly warned the West that they are being deceived by the Russians and their apparent desire for 'co-existence'.

On a number of occasions I have been in the Russian Orthodox Church and Convent of the Garden of Geth- semane. It is full of icons, has a dark precious filtered light and smells of incense. With my very different spiritual background I imagined that there was not much spiritual life there. During the war however, I discovered that one of the greatest saints in the Middle East is the Abbess of that Convent.

Mother Barbara is in her eighties, and is a most remarkable Christian saint. She is one of the only two people I know in Israel who had any sense that in 1973 a terrible catastrophe was about to fall upon the nation. Every time that she had begun to pray for the country, during her prayer watches, she found herself in tears. This had so troubled her that she had consulted one of her superiors. He said 'Well, my dear, you are getting old, and when one is getting old one more easily weeps.' Unable to accept this explanation, however she said later to a friend 'I do not believe it is so. Some terrible catastrophe is hanging over us.' She proved to be right.

Mother Barbara told me about prophecies which she had heard in Russia back in 1911. During the political upheavals of that time her father was in danger of his life from several quarters. She feared that he was in imminent danger so she went to a monastery many miles north of Moscow, where she knew there were godly monks and asked them to pray for her father's safety. As a result of their prayer, Mother Barbara believes that her father and her family were among the few allowed out of Russia at that time. Mother Barbara went to Jerusalem where she has lived ever since. She told me that when the monks were praying for her father, one of them had prophesied and that she had written it all down.

She brought out an old tattered notebook and began translating parts of the prophecy from Russian: 'An evil will shortly take Russia and wherever this evil comes, rivers of blood will flow. This evil will take the whole world and wherever it goes, rivers of blood will flow because of it. It is not the Russian soul, but an imposition on the Russian soul. It is not an ideology, or a philosophy, but a spirit from hell. In the last days Germany will be divided in two. France will just be nothing. Italy will be judged by natural disasters. Britain will lose her empire and all her colonies and will come to almost total ruin, but will be saved by praying women. America will feed the world, but will finally collapse. Russia and China will destroy each other. Finally Russia will be free and from her, believers will go forth and turn many from the nations to God.' The old monk then said to her, 'You will live to see Russia free, but you will not live to see the Antichrist.'

Once again I should say that we must not gullibly swallow all of this. We should consider it carefully, testing everything. Nevertheless I do think that these words are quite remarkable. In 1911, who ever would have thought that some crackpot little movement in Russia would rule a very large part of the earth and that Marxism would become the most powerful force in the 20th Century world? Who would have thought that Germany would be divided in two, or that Britain, then a very strong nation, would lose her empire and all her colonies, and almost come to ruin? Who would have believed that America would be feeding the world? In 1911, who would have imagined that Russia and China could be capable of destroying each other? Remember that China had only the weakest of governments at that time. If the monk had said that Russia and Japan would destroy each other, that would have been a possibility for Japan had defeated Russia in the Russo-Japanese War of 1904–5 and was a growing military power in the Far East.

While I was in Israel during the Yom Kippur War, I had the strong feeling that I was seeing a cameo of what would happen just as suddenly to the Free World. Just as that assault came unexpectedly, so one day we would wake up to find that we were being attacked on all fronts. I believe that the next blow-up in Israel could indeed involve the whole world in a very short space of time. Many people think that if we have a third world war, it could all be over in a few weeks. This could be the case, but in that short time a tremendous amount could have happened. If there were a collision between the United States and Russia over Israel, China could take the opportunity of attacking Russia in the back.

Thus we could have half the world locked in conflict within a matter of days.

Within weeks Europe could be occupied and freed, Russia devastated, and China laid waste and the political systems centred in them destroyed. Very much of what we now call civilization would then be in ruins. Out of such catastrophe could come a period of unparalleled gospel opportunity. It would be opportunity unprecedented in the last 2,000 years, because the world would be in pieces and there would be a moral vacuum. The church of God could have possibilities for preaching and teaching such as she has never known. Then I believe that after a decade or two at the most, there would emerge a strong world government, the subsequent rise of a so-called man of peace, the Antichrist, and the final events of world history. In my view, although a speculative view, it is a real possibility. When we come to the clear statements of God's Word we are on a firm foundation. Above and beyond these, however, we must be very careful indeed and you will, of course, have to test it for yourself.

At this point someone is bound to ask, 'Will those of us who are Christians be there to see a third world war? Won't we have been taken up by our Lord?' I would ask them in reply, 'What authority have we in the Word of God for believing that a third world war will be the last?' There may be a fourth and fifth. I believe in a Rapture*, but I believe that it will come at the beginning of the Tribulation or during it, in other words at the very end of the age. I do not believe that we are at the very end yet, but that we are moving into the last phase and do not know how long we have left. What I am convinced of is that out of the chaos and destruction I have been describing will come the turning of the Jewish people to the Lord. That will be life from the dead referred to by Paul in Romans 11:15. The age-old aspiration of the Jewish people has been that ultimately the whole world would be blessed through them and that all nations would flow to Jerusalem. In the end the Jewish people will see that through the Messiah this has come to pass. They will see that from every nation there are those who are joined to the Messiah and that in him they have all been made one (Ephesians 2:11–18; 3:6).

Will Israel survive? There is no doubt about that. Whether

*See Appendix.

there is a limited but terrible Middle East war or a more widely spread nuclear confrontation, Israel will survive, for God has said so. Even if all the armies of the world were to gather against Israel, the Jewish people would not be annihilated. Neither will the land be taken away from them. Israel will more than survive. She will triumph. All that has been promised to her will be fulfilled.

7. What Next?

It is interesting to note that many of the major biblical signs have been fulfilled. Indeed all of those relating to Israel have been fulfilled in the last century, many during the last thirty years; namely, the return of the Jewish people to the Promised Land, the re-creation of the state of Israel, the possession and repopulating of the land, the rebuilding of the cities which for so many generations were desolate and the retaking of Jerusalem. There are, however, a number of prophecies which have yet to be fulfilled. We know that Israel and Jerusalem will be the focal point of much more conflict and that further war is predicted. We find some of these wars described in Ezekiel 38, 39; Joel 3; Zechariah 12, 14; Mark 13:14–23; and Revelation 16:16. Whether all these refer to one war or to different wars is debatable but it would seem to me that we have at least a few wars described here, still in Israel's future, and this I have discussed more fully in previous chapters.

It would also seem clear that Israel will eventually own much more territory than she has at present. Some believe that she will finally possess all that God promised to Abraham, that is 'from the wilderness to Lebanon, and from the river, the River Euphrates, as far as the Western Sea' (Deuteronomy 11:24, New American Standard Bible). It would appear from Isaiah 11:14 that Israel will possess the mountains of Lebanon, Edom, Ammon, and Moab, in other words all of present Jordan and a considerable part of southern Lebanon.

There is another apparently unfulfilled prophecy in Isaiah 19. In verses 23 to 25 it says, 'In that day there will be a highway from Egypt to Assyria, and the Assyrians will come into Egypt and the Egyptians into Assyria, and the Egyptians will worship with the Assyrians. In that day Israel will be the third party with Egypt and Assyria, a blessing in the midst of the earth, whom the Lord of hosts has blessed saying, "Blessed is Egypt My people, and Assyria the work of My hands, and Israel My inheritance" ' (New American Standard Bible). One view is that this will have its fulfilment in the Millennium,* another strongly held opinion is that it will be fulfilled before the Millennium. Many tend to think that anyone who recognizes the re-creation of the state of Israel as a fulfilment of God's word is of necessity anti-Arab. The fact is that Israel will, in the purpose of God, become the means of blessing salvation and security to the Arabs. In my estimation the present course of events in the Lebanon would have been very different if this one Christian state among the Arab nations had understood this.

A matter that many people raise in connection with the future of Israel is whether the temple will be rebuilt or not. This is based upon a number of Old Testament prophecies – for example Amos 9:11, Ezekiel 40–48 – and also New Testament references such as Matthew 24:15 ('the abomination of desolation ... standing in the holy place,' New American Standard Bible) and 2 Thessalonians 2:3, 4 ('the man of lawlessness ... takes his seat in the temple of God, displaying himself as being God,' New American Standard Bible).

There are some amazing stories about the rebuilding of the temple in circulation at the present time. Among the most crazy is the one about the stone being prepared in Indiana, U.S.A., for Israel has got marvellous stone of her own. Can you imagine orthodox Jewry ever accepting a temple built with American stone? Seriously there are some very real problems in connection with this whole matter of the temple. If it is to be rebuilt, are we going to have the reinstitution of the priesthood and of animal sacrifice? It seems to me unlikely that first we should have the symbol, then its fulfilment, then return to the symbol; first the shadow, then the substance, then the shadow again. Surely the Messiah has either fulfilled all this or he has not. Nowhere in Scripture does God speak of returning to the figure or shadow, once its fulfilment has come.

A practical difficulty would emerge because the priesthood was subject to very strict rules. If the priesthood were to be

*See appendix

reinstituted, how would Israel establish who was qualified for the office? One could take people whose name was Cohen, Khan, Cowan, or other variations on the same name 'Cohen,' which in Hebrew means 'priest,' since such Jewish names are a sure indication of descent from priestly families. But if there had been any intermarriage down through the years they would be disqualified. Are there many Cohens who are absolutely pure? Again one could find the Levites through such names as Levy, Levan, and so on, but there would be the same problem of purity. Neither can I believe that there will be a return to animal sacrifice. The vast majority of Jewish people would be wholly against this. It is precisely because of these problems that orthodox Jewry believes that only the Messiah himself can build the temple. Indeed the ultra-orthodox Hassids* of Jerusalem believe that the creation of the state of Israel is itself a sin. Until recently they would not even speak Hebrew except in worship preferring to speak Yiddish because of their belief based on Zephaniah 3:9 that only the Messiah could 'turn again a pure language.'

Nevertheless some people will refer to Ezekiel chapters 40 to 48 and other similar Scriptures as proof that the temple will be rebuilt. I am not convinced that these passages are speaking about a literal temple. I believe rather that they use symbolic language to speak of the spiritual and eternal house of God. Ezekiel's vision and John's vision in Revelation chapters 21 and 22 have striking similarities and are to be interpreted symbolically and not literally. Both speak of the eternal dwelling place of God not made with hands, but consisting of living stones. In other words believing Jews and believing Gentiles built together in Christ (Ephesians 2:11–22). Whether there is to be a literal rebuilding of the temple or not, we know that Christ is building the temple which is his church and the battle of the ages is over this (Matthew 16:18, cf. Ephesians 2: 19–21). I understand the reference to the offering up of sacrifices in the light of 1 Peter 2:5 'You also as living stones, are being built up as a spiritual house for a holy priesthood to offer up spiritual sacrifices acceptable to God through Jesus Christ' (New American Standard Bible).

Whatever happens in the immediate future, Israel will not only survive but she will also triumph. Far from being in the least bit afraid for her, I know she will come through

*See appendix.

victoriously. Meanwhile each new phase of strife will be but
another step in God's cornering of his people. He will corner
them in such a way that they will finally be driven to call
upon him. When this happens a spirit of supplication and
grace will be poured out upon them and they shall look to him
whom they pierced. There will be a mourning that will cover
the whole land, a bitterness of heart as for the death of a
firstborn son. (Read Zechariah 12:10.)   All Israel will
recognize the fact that she rejected her Messiah and was
party to his crucifixion. What a day that will be! It will not be
the kind of mourning that drove Judas to hang himself, but
the kind of mourning which Peter felt when, during his trial,
Jesus turned and looked at him. Peter went out and wept and
his was a repentance that led to restoration. This prophecy of
Zechariah emphasizes the sorrow and grief of heart on the
part of the whole nation and the wonderful reconciliation and
cleansing in which it will end. Zechariah 13:1. There will be
many tears then, which will melt the heart and warm the
spirit. When this happens to the Jewish people it will be life
from the dead for the whole Church.

There are diametrically opposed views among evangelicals
about the state of the Church at the end of the age. There are
those who do not believe that there will be a great revival and
awakening. Such people remind us that the Lord said, 'When
the Son of Man cometh, shall he find faith on the earth?'
(Luke 18:8, The Authorized version), and 'the love of many
shall wax cold' (Matthew 24:12). There is also the verse in 2
Thessalonians 2:3 which says, 'That day shall not come,
except there come a falling away first'. The opposite view,
also based on Scripture, is that at the end there will be a great
outpouring of the Spirit of God. We are told, for instance,
that the prophecy of Joel was not completely fulfilled on the
Day of Pentecost and that it awaits a final fulfilment. Those
holding this view look for a great awakening, for 'latter rain,'
for 'multitudes in the valley of decision.' I am not sure that
these views are irreconcilable.

My own view is that the complement to the Day of
Pentecost will be the taking away of the veil from the hearts
of the Jewish people. I believe that this divine triumph will
show itself in a tremendous release of resurrection life and
power into the whole Church. It will indeed be 'life from the
dead' (Romans 11:15). It is a thrilling prospect. Pentecost

was itself 'life from the dead.' It was the resurrection, life and power of the ascended Christ, given to and manifested in all those he had saved by the person of the Holy Spirit. That 'life from the dead' was to take the Church through its early days until the gospel was preached to the ends of the Roman Empire and beyond. The apostles who first preached that gospel were all Jewish so it seems to me that it would be a most wonderful thing if at the end of the age, it were once again those in Christ, in the Messiah, of Jewish background, who were to become the dynamic to carry the whole Body of Christ through the last phase of history.

8. Facing the Future

The time has now come for those of us who know the Lord Jesus Christ as Lord and Saviour to face up to reality. It may cost us very much to do so but however costly this is, in the end we shall not regret it. To live in a spiritual fantasy may be enjoyable for the present, but will not carry us through the day of crisis. In the final analysis it is a matter of spiritual foundations, a subject about which the Bible has much to say. Christ's words in Luke 6:46–49 are very relevant here: 'Why do you call me, "Lord, Lord" and do not do what I say? Everyone who comes to me and hears my words and acts upon them, I will show you whom he is like: he is like a man building a house who dug deep and laid a foundation upon the rock and when a flood arose the river burst against that house and could not shake it, because it had been well built. But the one who has heard and has not acted accordingly is like a man who built a house upon the ground without any foundation and the river burst against it and immediately it collapsed and the ruin of that house was great' (New American Standard Bible). The Lord Jesus himself pointed out that it is not good enough for us merely to hear his words, or even to recognize them as truth. That in itself will not save us from collapse in the day of trial. We have to face up to the truth, face reality and its implications for us and act accordingly.

I have been a Christian for over twenty-five years and in that time I have heard numerous references to the fact that we shall see much war and trouble at the end of the age. I have yet to meet a true evangelical who does not believe that the last phase will be marked by wars, great upheavals and breakdown on every level of life. On the other hand, all of us are loath to believe that any of this could be on our doorsteps. The fact that the matter of prophecy and the end time has become the subject for wild predictions, unbalanced views and even extreme actions, only makes us more cautious than ever. Sometimes when such predictions or views are shown to be invalid by the passage of time, we tend to become cynical in our attitude to the whole matter. Nevertheless God's word will be fulfilled and I am sure that when these things eventually occur, a large number of us will be taken by surprise. One of the most painful experiences for us as the people of God is to suddenly realize that what we have believed in theory for years might actually be about to happen. For then comes the distress of facing up to all our frittering away of time and money and our engagement in so much useless activity.

Someone said to me some while ago that we Christians so believe that trouble is coming that we are immunized to it. We tend to assume that just because we believe that it will come, we are automatically prepared for it. The contrary however, can be true; such a mentality in fact could leave us totally unprepared. The only answer is to face reality with living faith.

It is interesting to note that when the Lord Jesus speaks about the signs of his coming in Matthew 24 and 25, he addresses his remarks particularly to the most responsible of his servants, although of course his words have relevance for all true believers. This point is often overlooked. He speaks for example, of the 'master of the house' (Matthew 24:43) and of 'the faithful and wise servant' who has been set over the household with responsibility to feed the other servants (Matthew 24:45). He also speaks of 'ten virgins', all of whom held a responsible position in connection with the coming wedding. To all of these servants, the most responsible in his work, he says, 'Be ye also ready: for in such an hour as ye think not the Son of man cometh' (Matthew 24:44 Authorized version). And, 'Watch therefore; for ye know neither the day nor the hour wherein the Son of man cometh' (Matthew 25:13 Authorized version).

We would have expected that if anyone was ready, it would have been such responsible servants of the Lord. This only serves to emphasize the need for all of us to be ready — for his coming and for trials that come our way. I have already mentioned that of all the Christians whom I know in Israel, only two had any inkling of the coming trouble in the months preceding the Yom Kippur War. It is a sobering fact that the Lord told us not only to pray, but to watch and pray.

Many Christians, when thinking about the prospect of predicted persecution, worldwide strife, or economic ills, with the attendant loss of jobs and well-being are filled with great fear. Unintentionally perhaps, we have in reading the Bible, selected passages of joy and comfort and not faced the implications of the parts concerning persecution and wars. Sometimes we accept certain truths in theory without ever having faced up to the implications. If we become excessively fearful it must surely mean that we are in fact finding it difficult to face up to such implications.

It is no answer to ignore these matters. However if these things come to pass and take the people for whom I am responsible by surprise, they will not thank me for having given them sweet words when I ought to have been warning them. There is a sense in which it would be far better for us to have our fear now and be done with it, than suddenly to panic when these things actually begin to happen.

We must see through the negative to the positive, for in fact, the future for believers is tremendously exciting. Our Lord Jesus did not say, 'Be fearful at the prospect of these things.' He said, 'When these things begin to come to pass, then look up and lift up your heads; for your redemption draweth nigh' (Luke 21:28, Authorized version). He described our future in four words: 'Your redemption draweth nigh.' I believe that we have a tremendous future. There are those who believe that all Christians will soon be taken up by Jesus to be with him. Praise God if that is so, and though I believe that it will probably be a little longer than they think, if I am mistaken about this, so much the better.

The fact of the matter is that our Lord Jesus commanded us to 'look up and lift up our heads.' That is the only antidote to fear. If we look down, we shall be fearful. If we look around, we shall be fearful. Only by looking up and seeing that the Lord Jesus is enthroned at the right hand of the Father with all authority in heaven and on earth shall we become full of hope and joy. We have been told to be ready although we do not know exactly when our Lord will come and readiness involves facing up to reality. No one can hope to be ready unless he faces the facts of the situation. We must therefore wake up to the facts or we stand to lose very much.

The Lord told us to watch and pray, not merely to pray. The word 'watch' means to keep awake or to be alert and is relevant for us today. We need to keep awake and alive to all that is happening and turn it into prayer. It is interesting to note that our Lord told us to 'keep alert at all times, praying in order that you may have strength to escape all these things that are about to take place, and to stand before the Son of man' (Luke 21:36, New American Standard Bible). With reference to the final phase of the end, he also told us to 'pray that your flight may not be in the winter, or on a Sabbath' (Matthew 24:20 New American Standard Bible). In other words, our prayer is to be intensely practical. On a different level, the Lord wants us to enter into that realm of prayer until, by his Spirit, we see his purpose fulfilled and realized.

The present moving of the Holy Spirit renewing believers all over the world, bringing back worship as a living reality and giving practical expression to our oneness in Christ, must among other things, produce a dynamic ministry of intercession. It cannot be right to make an experience of the Holy Spirit a means of escapism. We cannot escape our responsibilities and any thought of self sacrifice by simply enjoying ourselves and idling away the time while the whole world teeters on the brink of disaster. The Spirit of God would lead us not only to an understanding of the Church as the body of Christ, but to a deep costly self sacrificing intercession.

The trouble with most Christians today is that we stop praying where believers in the Bible began, by which I mean that usually when we find out what the will of God is about a matter, we thank him and stop praying, but Daniel for example, when he found out that the seventy years of captivity were about to be fulfilled and that he was living in those very days, began to pray three times a day for its realization. (See Daniel 9:1–3.) If God had already revealed to Jeremiah that there were seventy years of captivity, surely in the sovereignty of God it would finish at the end of that time, whether Daniel prayed or not. Here we face the mystery of prayer. For we can pray into being what God has said he will himself do sovereignly. Satan became so disturbed by Daniel's prayer that he sought to destroy him in the lions' den, but Daniel came out of the den to fulfil his prayer ministry. This is the type of prayer we need to learn about. If we believe that God has said something about Israel, about the veil being taken away from the Jewish heart and about the Church of God in the time of the end, we need, by the Spirit, to pray his purpose into fulfilment.

Israel has never been in such need of prayer as she is today. It is interesting to note the exhortation to 'pray for the peace of Jerusalem' (Psalm 122:6, Authorized version) and the promise that follows it: 'they shall prosper that love thee.' Although it is undoubtedly correct to interpret this in terms of the spiritual Jerusalem ('the Jerusalem which is above') and to pray for the peace and the building up of the people of God, God's spiritual Zion, it also has a physical and literal application. It is interesting to see how that application has come into its own in the last twenty-eight years. The peace of the whole world, moreover, is increasingly dependent upon the peace of Jerusalem.

It is even more interesting to note the principle contained in the promise, 'they shall prosper that love thee' for such scriptures as Zechariah 12 make it clear that God will judge every nation by its attitude to Israel. Nations that compromise over Israel will themselves be compromised; those that seek to break Israel will themselves be broken and nations that go against Israel will be opposed by God. This is again clearly stated by God in Isaiah 60:12, 'that nation and kingdom that will not serve thee shall perish, yea those nations shall be utterly wasted.' In Jeremiah 30:11, the Lord states the matter even more emphatically, 'for I am with thee, saith the Lord, to save thee: though I will make a full end of all nations whither I have scattered thee, yet will I not make a full end of thee.' There is a tremendous need for the godly Christian remnant in the nations to intercede, not only for Israel but for the nations in which they are found. Many nations of the world, apart from the Communist bloc, are ripe for judgment. The cup of their iniquity is already full. By their immorality and lawlessness, their bloodguiltiness in the matter of abortion, their despising of the name and word of God and their attitude to Israel, they have prepared themselves for the judgment of God. Those of us who see this should turn to God with all our hearts and make supplication for ourselves and for our nation. We should intercede with God that he might show mercy in days of wrath. We need mighty preachers of righteousness and fearless prophets who will turn many people and even nations to God in these last days. This can only be as there are true persevering intercessors.

Towards the end of 1973, a Dutch Reformed minister had a dream in which he saw a square in Utrecht, a town in Holland. On one side of this square stands an ancient statue of Willibrord mounted on a horse. He was the man responsible for bringing the gospel to Holland at the end of the seventh century. On the other side of the same square is a much smaller and more beautiful statue of Anna Frank, the young Jewish girl who died in the concentration camp at Belsen and whose diary has since moved the hearts of millions.

In his dream the minister saw Willibrord dismount, cross the square to Anna Frank and take her up in his arms. He then turned round and started to carry her back to his horse. As he walked across the square, however, his steps became slower and slower until he could go no further. Anna Frank had become too heavy for him. Then to his amazement Anna Frank began to carry Willibrord. He understood from his dream that God was saying that if Holland stood by Israel whatever the cost, in the end Israel would be the salvation of Holland. This dream illustrates a vital truth which applies to both nations, and individuals — 'they shall prosper that love thee.' Therefore what we need today is a reality produced in us by the Holy Spirit, which will enable us to face the future. We need to be prepared both personally and corporately as the people of God, for those things which are coming upon the earth. Furthermore we need to be equipped spiritually, for God needs men and women saved by his grace, in union with Christ, anointed by his Spirit, who can 'rule nations' from the secret place. God now seeks as in the days of Ezekiel, 'for a man among them, that should build up the wall and stand in the gap for the land, that I should not destroy it.' Ezekiel 22:30. May we all be such intercessors.

9. God's Purpose in Israel ✳

Monday · 27/6/83

There are some Christians who say that there is no further place for the Jew in God's programme. They argue that all unfulfilled Biblical prophecy about Israel is really for the Church and that the Jewish people are permanently under the wrath of God. On the other hand there are others who give to the Jew such a unique and exalted position that it makes you wonder why you are a Christian. Would it not be better after all to be a Jew? Between these two extreme points of view many Christians flounder for there appears to be so much Scripture to support them both. The more one listens to one point of view, the more one is convinced by it. Then one hears the other view and it appears equally convincing. This confusion begins to disappear once we examine the heart of the matter and see the purpose of God for the Jewish people. We must ask ourselves therefore what that purpose is.

When God chose Abraham out of all the men on the earth it was because he wished to form a people to be his dwelling place, through whom the light of God should shine into the darkest and most remote parts of the earth. It was not that the Jewish people should become merely a separated people but that they should be the vessel to take the salvation of God to all the nations. The wonder of it all is that this was finally accomplished not despite their fall but through it. Rom. 11:11 states that 'through their fall salvation is come unto the Gentiles' (Authorized version). Their calling was never meant to be an end in itself but rather the glorious means by which the knowledge of God should cover the earth as the waters cover the sea. The temptation of the Jewish people to make their divine election and calling an end in itself has been present from the beginning of their history and was consequently a major concern of all the prophets.

One of the main reasons for the book of Jonah being

written was over this concern. The prophet Jonah was in fact
himself guilty of this kind of false particularism which
thought of everything outside the covenant people as
'uncircumcision' and therefore outside the interest of God
apart from judgment. When therefore he heard the voice of
God in one of his 'quiet times' saying 'Jonah, I want you to go
to Nineveh' he became very confused. Why bother to warn
them of judgment and perhaps give them the opportunity to
repent? Jonah was in a theological straitjacket of his own
making and could not have escaped from it, even if he had
wanted to. Jonah could not face up to the challenge of God's
call and ran away from it. He booked a passage on a boat
going as far from Nineveh as possible and tried to put as
much distance as he could between that city and himself, but
God intervened by preparing a great fish and then using a
great storm. In the belly of the fish Jonah remembered
Solomon's prayer at the dedication of the temple. He
repented and prayed and the Lord heard him and delivered
him. (See Jonah 2, especially v.4; cf. I Kings 8:22–53.)

When Jonah finally arrived in Nineveh, he delivered God's
message with all the energy he could muster. It was a message
of judgment and it perfectly matched Jonah's own feelings
about what that city deserved. It was one of the greatest
shocks of his life when all the Ninevites from the king
downwards repented, even to the point of dressing the
domestic animals in sackcloth. As a result of this God
deferred his judgment on the city for a generation but Jonah
as one might expect, was very angry indeed – 'it displeased
Jonah exceedingly.'

We can see ourselves in Jonah. He was the prisoner of his
own theology. As is so often the case when our ideas run
counter to God's Plan and our conceptions receive a divine
blow, he fell into a deep depression and went away sulking.
The last straw was when the Lord allowed a gourd to grow up to
shade him and then let it die within a day. God however was
in the whole thing. He prepared the gourd, he prepared the
worm that killed it and he prepared the sultry east wind that
caused Jonah to faint. It is interesting that Jonah went out of
the city not because he wanted to die – that came later– but because he could not face up to the possibility that his conceptions were wrong. He went out to wait for the Lord to change
his mind and come round to a more sensible way of thinking.

As Jonah was sullen over the death of the gourd, God
came to him and said, 'Jonah, you have had more
compassion on that gourd that grew overnight and perished
overnight than you have had upon the whole city of Nineveh.
How can I destroy this great city? Should I not show
compassion to the 120,000 little children so young that they
do not know their left hand from their right and to the
many animals?' We ought to remember when we are tempted
to judge the reluctant prophet that it took a great man to
leave the book of Jonah where the author did. If I had been
writing my autobiography containing this story I would have
added another short paragraph: 'Jonah turned again to the
Lord and saw the purpose of God in the calling of his people.'
Jonah was so dealt with however that he could leave the
account where he did so that ever afterwards people could
speak about his hardness. He left us with a message.

Why did God choose Israel? Jonah learned the hard way
that Israel's calling was to save Nineveh not to damn it. Her
vocation was to take the knowledge of God to Nineveh, not
to withhold it from her. Of course if you had spoken to
Jonah, he would have said, 'If they all want to come up to
Jerusalem and get converted, that is all right. We will accept
them after we have examined them.' God however, knew the
streets of Nineveh as well as he knew the streets of Jerusalem.
He knew the number of young children and babies living
there. He even cared about the domestic animals there. That
God was so concerned for Nineveh came as a shock to
Jonah. The Lord will not judge even a heathen city without
first warning it. What a revelation we have here of the
character and nature of God. He has never judged a nation or
a city or even a system without first warning them. Sometimes
Christians make God appear to be a kind of divine machine
with reactions and responses more like those of an electronic
brain than of a person. We must remember that God is both
light and love and that it pains him to have to judge. God
does not delight in judgment but in mercy. He has no dark
and terrible propensity for wrath and destruction. When
finally he judges it is with grief.

Would that the Jewish people had forever learnt the lesson
that Jonah learnt, for God had a purpose for his people that
was not fulfilled by them. Moreover Jonah was used by God
to deliver Nineveh from judgment only after spending three

days in the great fish. That is why our Lord spoke of the sign of Jonah the prophet (Matthew 12:38–41). Jonah symbolizes the death, burial and resurrection of the Messiah because only through the Lord Jesus could this original purpose of God for his people be fulfilled. Only through the Messiah and his work at Calvary could the salvation of God be carried to the ends of the earth and an innumerable multitude from every tongue and tribe and nation come into the commonwealth of Israel.

There has been such tragic ignorance as to the purpose of God in the election and divine calling of Israel. Here the interpretation of Romans 9–11 is of fundamental importance. Are these chapters a mere parenthesis in the Apostle's tremendous argument, a kind of heavenly digression with real value but distinct from his main line of thought? Paul has been unfolding the whole counsel of God concerning the believer's standing in Christ and has concluded with the tremendous statement contained in Romans 8:39 that there is nothing which can separate us from the love of God in him. Does he then suddenly shoot off at a tangent only to come back to his original theme in Romans 12:1: 'I beseech you therefore, brethren, by the mercies of God ....' Does the 'therefore' in chapter 12 refer back to only the first eight chapters of the book rather than to the whole eleven? Or is the Apostle Paul by the Spirit of God, taking us into the holiest of all to face that which lies behind our 'so great salvation?' All agree that the subject matter of Romans 9–11 is predestination and election, however they may further interpret the passage. The fact that the Israel of God is at the very heart of these chapters must surely make us ask ourselves whether there can be two elect peoples, or whether God has not been forming one elect people from the time he chose and called Abraham. It is interesting to note that even under the old covenant we have some remarkable examples of Gentiles being introduced to God's elect people e.g. Ruth, Bathsheba, Rahab etc.

In my opinion there is only one elect people. The problem is that we tend to think of them as Gentiles, or very largely so. God however sees the whole matter from a different vantage point. His word states that Abraham is the father of all who believe (Rom. 4:11, 12; Galatians 3:7, 29) and that every Gentile who believes is incorporated into the commonwealth of Israel. The Lord Jesus stated that 'salvation is of the Jews'

(John 4:22). Thus it is not a matter of the believing Jew coming to the Christian, but of his coming into the Messiah, in the same way the believing Gentile has come.

Paul pursues this line of thought in Ephesians 2:11–16: 'Therefore remember that at one time you Gentiles in the flesh, called the uncircumcision by what is called the circumcision, which is made in the flesh by hands – remember that you were at that time separated from Christ, alienated from the commonwealth of Israel and strangers to the covenants of promise, having no hope and without God in the world. But now in Christ Jesus you who once were far off have been brought near in the blood of Christ. For he is our peace, who has made us both one and has broken down the dividing wall of hostility, by abolishing in his flesh the law of commandments and ordinances, that he might create in himself one new man in place of the two, so making peace and might reconcile us both to God in one body through the cross, thereby bringing the hostility to an end' (Revised Standard version). Again in Ephesians 3:6: he says, 'the Gentiles are fellow heirs, members of the same body and partakers of the promise in Christ Jesus through the gospel' (Revised Standard version). (See also Galatians 3:28.) It is in the Messiah that the two become one.

In Romans 11, the Apostle Paul speaks of an olive tree. He says in verses 17 and 18: 'But if some of the branches were broken off and you being a wild olive, were grafted in among them and became partaker with them of the rich root of the olive tree, do not be arrogant toward the branches; but if you are arrogant, remember that it is not you who supports the root, but the root supports you' (New American Standard Bible). The natural branches, the unbelieving Jews were broken off and the wild olive branches the believing Gentiles, were grafted in. This is emphasized by the words 'became partaker with them of the rich root of the olive tree.' What does 'grafted in among them' and 'partaker with them' mean here? To whom does the word 'them' refer? Note also that it is not 'you' (i.e. the believing Gentile) who supports the root, but the root supports 'you.' What is the root which carries the innumerable multitude of the redeemed since Calvary? It surely speaks of the Messiah who is the root of Jesse (Isaiah 11:10; cf. Romans 15:12), as well as the offspring of Jesse. That is why the Lord Jesus could say, 'before Abraham was I am' (John 8:58).

It therefore surely means that Abraham, Isaac, Jacob, Moses, David, Isaiah, Jeremiah, Zechariah etc. are the stock which carries you. You are not carrying them, you are grafted in with them and you have become partakers with them. See Ephesians 2:19; Hebrews 11:39, 40; Matthew 8:11, 12; Revelation 21:12, 14. (Note the names of the twelve patriarchs and of the twelve apostles, representing the elect people of God from both covenants, built into the one city of God.) See also Hebrews 11:10, 16; 12:22; 13:14; Galatians 4:26. The key to all this is that all the redeemed of God have been brought into the commonwealth of Israel.

The answer to this whole matter lies in what it means to be 'one man in the Messiah.' Is the Jew saved in a different way from the Gentile, or is he also saved through the blood of the Messiah? The fact is that there is only one work of redemption through which both Jew and Gentile are saved. Furthermore a careful reading of the New Testament brings us to the conclusion that the true believer whether Jew or Gentile, is found in Christ, that is in the Messiah. For the true believer, everything is provided in the Messiah. It is in fact very helpful to our understanding when reading the Scriptures to substitute the Hebrew word 'Messiah' for its Greek equivalent 'Christ.' Even the nickname 'Christian' (Acts 11:26) only means 'Christ's ones' or 'Messiah's ones.'

This whole matter is set in proper perspective by the phrase in Romans 11:24, 'be grafted into their *own* olive tree.' If I understand the Apostle Paul clearly, the church of God is 'their *own* olive tree'. It does not matter how many countless millions of Gentiles have been saved by the grace of God, they are all found in that olive tree. Those 'wild olive branches' may extend to the ends of the earth yet they do not bear the tree. It is the root that bears them.

It may help us in our understanding of this whole matter to suppose for a moment that the Jewish people had received the Messiah instead of rejecting him. Let us imagine that the entire nation had acclaimed him as the Messianic King, as the Saviour and deliverer of his people. Notwithstanding he would still have had to die, for it was the only way in which fallen man could be saved. Christ's death was foreordained. Sooner or later knowing the power of evil there would have been a confrontation with the Roman Empire and they would have crucified this Jewish king. It would then have been only the gentile world that would have executed Christ. The whole Jewish people would have understood that it was the Lamb of God who had died and that his death was the fulfilment of all that the sacrifices under the old covenant symbolized. They would have understood the full meaning of that which the prophets had spoken when they foretold not only the glory and kingdom of the Messiah but his sufferings and death for the people. They would have experienced the salvation of God through his death and resurrection. By the empowering of the Spirit of God they would have gone out to the ends of the earth proclaiming this salvation which was not only for them but for the whole world. What then would have happened to the countless thousands of Gentiles who would have been saved through their preaching? By believing in the Messiah who was wholly Jewish according to the flesh, they would have become Jews through conversion. Thus the whole matter would have been rightly seen as the fulfilment of Jewish history and of the hopes and aspirations centred for example in such prophecies as Psalm 72; Isaiah 2; 62; and Zech 8. They would have seen the salvation of God going to the ends of the earth as the fulfilment of the promise that the Lord made to Abraham 'in thee shall all the families of the earth be blessed' Gen. 12:3. No doubt many of those Gentiles who would have rejected the Messiah would still have nicknamed converted Gentiles along with believing Jews as 'Messiah's ones' that is 'Christians' but would have rightly understood them all as being Jewish.

Alas the Jewish people as a whole did not recognize and receive their Messiah and thus began the anguished history of their dispersion. Salvation at that time came only to a minority of the Jewish people. We should remember of course, that in O.T. history, it had often only been a small minority that knew a living relationship to God. At one time Elijah literally thought that he was the only one left. Salvation in fact did not come automatically to every circumcised Jew but only to those who had a true relationship, through faith, with the living God. This is Paul's argument in Romans, chapters 4 and 9. He says that 'they are not all Israel who are of Israel.' In other words, within the outward covenant people of God were those who were the elect people of God. All were circumcised but for those who were truly saved it was not a mere outward conforming to the law but a keeping of the divine covenant through faith. When the Messiah born of that stock,· appeared on the scene, the nation's establishment rejected him. They were circumcised but certainly not saved, as for example Annas or Caiaphas. Yet in the most amazing way their rejection brought about the redeeming purpose of God (Acts 2:23; 4:27, 28).

The first people to be saved in New Testament times were as far as we know, all Jewish and with the possible exception of Luke, all the divinely inspired writers of the New Testament were Jewish believers. We have therefore the outward people of God, Israel and within that people the true Israel of God. These were the natural branches which were never broken off. The Apostle Paul says in Romans 11:7, 'the election obtained it and the rest were hardened.' These are hard words but nevertheless, the word of God.

We must note that in Romans 11:20, it is stated that the natural branches which were broken off were removed because of unbelief. Similarly the wild olive branches were grafted in because of God-given faith. In other words all who are in this olive tree are there by faith. This all adds up to the simple fact that while the New Testament declares dogmatically that there is a new man, a new creation in the Messiah, Gentile believers have come into something which has its roots in the old covenant and is the glorious fulfilment of it.

There has been a drastic change from the New Testament outlook that a Jew when he became a follower of Yeshua (Jesus), maintained his Jewishness and his Jewish culture. Today a Jew who becomes such a follower of Yeshua is identified as a Christian. According to many Christians moreover, the loss of his Jewishness and separation from his Jewish culture is intrinsic to that identification. I think that this is very sad. Of course there are some who go too far the other way. They are so over-anxious to keep their Jewish identity that they contradict their standing in the Messiah. The whole point is that when a Jew is born again he really becomes a fulfilled Jew. Whether you call him a Jewish Christian, a Messianic believer, a follower of Yeshua or Jesus, or a Hebrew believer, he has been fulfilled. Such a one has come into the Messiah so long promised and has thus fulfilled God's original calling.

There are of course problems here such as that of circumcision, keeping the law, adhering to kosher laws, and so on. These problems far from being new are precisely those which faced the early church. Indeed these very problems were the occasion for much of the teaching in the New Testament, especially in the Epistles. Look for instance at Colossians 2:16ff. and Romans 14:5, 6. Paul's argument is this: 'If one man wants to keep a particular day as holy and another man wants to keep every day as holy, that is all right; if one man feels that he ought not to eat meat, or he observes certain food laws and another feels himself free from such laws, that's all right too, but such views either for or against must not be made the ground for division.' The fact is that this problem had caused a certain amount of division in the early church and it was this that the Apostle was seeking to correct. If my dietary law separates me from my fellow-believers, it is wrong. Upon the matter of circumcision the Apostle was even more adamant. (See his letter to the Galatians.) It is interesting to see that these New Testament problems are again becoming problems in our own day.

When a Jew becomes a Christian he has been born again into the elect people of God and has come into the Messiah and into his oneness. There is however, no reason why he should culturally lose his Jewishness. He is still a Jew in the same way that other Christians are still British or Chinese or American. He should not feel more alienated from his fellow Jews than others do from their fellow Britishers, fellow Chinese, or fellow Americans. It is the making of our race, of our nationality, or of our culture the ground for division which is wrong (Colossians 3: 10, 11), but we are not expected to shed all of our cultural heritage. Nevertheless, Paul saw that in Christ there is a new creation. The old has passed away, everything has become new (2 Corinthians 5:17). All the redeemed whether Jew or Gentile, have in the Messiah been separated unto God. Often the oneness a believing Jew has with believers of a Gentile background alienates him from his fellow Jews. If the reason for this is because a Jewish Christian rejects completely his cultural background, it is an unnecessary loss. If it is for the sake of Messiah, it is a necessary cost. In this right sense we all know a division from the world and a being joined to God.

It was believing Jews who first became what we call the Church of God. They were the true Israel of God. The majority of the Jewish people however, remained unbelievers and were therefore distinct from this. They went on to their sad and anguished history and the Church moved on to become increasingly composed of those with Gentile background. It seems to me quite clear from the word of God that in our day we are going to see the two lines come together again. Israel is being forced into a place where she will turn to God and as she turns to God she will recognize her Messiah.

Already I find more and more educated Jews beginning to consider Jesus. In Jewish thought right down the years the cross of Christ has represented everything unlovely and cruel, for so much evil has been perpetrated upon the Jewish people in the name of Christ and his Gospel. For the Jew therefore, the cross has been the symbol of persecution, hatred and injustice. Since the creation of the modern-day state of Israel however, there has been a growing change of attitude. Jewish people are beginning to look at Jesus more honestly. Here is the beginning of a genuine inquiry. In the days ahead I believe we are going to see a great many Jews born again through the power of God. We have therefore, a glorious future in front of us. I believe that something remarkable is going to happen with Israel before the coming of the Lord. It seems to me that we are going to see the counterpart of Pentecost at the end of the age.

Sometimes we Christians forget that in the wise and never-failing counsels of God, the falling away of the Jewish people played a definite role. For as things were, the Gentiles could never have been reached and brought into God's eternal purpose and saving grace but by the ending of Jewish nationhood and their dispersion. We also forget that we have been brought into something which has its root in the Old Testament and which carries everything that has followed. Some people would like us to dismiss almost all that happened in the Old Testament. For them the New Testament is everything and does not need the Old Testament. Apart from it being a good illustration book, they consider it a kind of prehistoric and useless appendage. What God did in the New Testament they say, is something altogether separate, which can and does stand on its own. For instance, there is the view that the Church, the Body of Christ, is an entirely New Testament concept which has nothing to do with the Old Testament and was a kind of divine after-thought when the Jewish people failed. This is however, taking the matter too far. The entire Old Testament looks forward to the New Testament and finds in it its fulfilment. The people of God under the old covenant were as much a part of what God has been doing throughout history as we are. They and we are one, the elect people of God.

The glorious truth is that when the predestinating power and grace of God has drawn in the fulness of the Gentiles, then that hardening which has befallen Israel will be removed with the most wonderful results. Those who begin to understand all this even faintly, realize that they are face to face with the mystery of election, the purpose of him who works all things after the counsel of his own will. This is beyond the comprehension of our finite minds to unravel. It was the full impact of this mystery upon Paul that made him cry out, 'How unsearchable are his judgments, and his ways past finding out' (Romans 11:33, 34, Authorized version).

The history of God's people is not some hopeless jumble, neither is the rejection and judgment of the Jewish nation with all the ensuing sorrow, suffering and break-up. It is part of a divine plan, mysterious and in many ways inexplicable. Yet God is its source, its guide and its goal. From the beginning of prophetic ministry there had been that clear understanding that the Jewish people were destined to bring the nations to God. The incredible truth is that this plan of God has been fulfilled through their fall. When the purpose of God to draw in the Gentiles has been accomplished, the veil on the Jewish heart will be removed with the most glorious consequences. Then the anguished suffering and incessant sorrow of the last two thousand years will give way to radiant glory and blessing. The end will finally be the bride of the Messiah, the wife of the Lamb, the New Jerusalem in the light of which the nations will walk. For the fulness of the Gentiles and the fulness of the Jews will have been brought into one body in the Messiah, where there is neither Jew nor Gentile, but the Messiah is everything in everyone. The dimensions of this purpose of God seem so vast, so mysterious and so invincibly powerful that we are silenced by the realization of our ignorance.

What we do know is that if the fall of the Jewish people meant the unsearchable riches of Christ for the Gentiles, what can their restoration mean but even greater fulness? If their casting away meant reconciliation for the Gentile world, their being received again will surely be life from the dead. It will be nothing less than the completion of the mystery of God. The prospect is so marvellous, so filled with glory, so utterly commensurate with the grace and character of the God we know, that it is no wonder that Paul breaks forth into his paean of praise: 'Oh, what a wonderful God we have! How great are his wisdom and knowledge and riches! How impossible it is for us to understand his decisions and his methods! For who among us can know the mind of the Lord? Who knows enough to be his counsellor and guide? And who could ever offer to the Lord enough to induce him to act? For everything comes from God alone. Everything lives by his power and everything is for his glory. To him be glory evermore' (Romans 11:33–36, The Living Bible).

10. From the Fig Tree Learn its Lesson

What did Christ mean when he said, 'From the fig tree learn its lesson' (Mark 13:28, Revised Standard version), or 'Learn the parable from the fig tree' (New American Standard Bible)?

The word translated 'lesson' in the Revised Standard Version is the same word that is often elsewhere translated in that version as 'parable.' Indeed when Luke records this statement, he uses the word in such a way that the Revised Standard Version has to translate it as 'parable.' (See Luke 21:29.) Was Jesus using the fig tree merely as an illustration or parable of coming summer as some would have us believe, or did his use of it have deeper meaning and significance?

It seems to me that the very way in which Christ draws our attention to the fig tree has more than the normal significance. We must remember that Mark chapters 11 to 13 cover the passage of two days. In Mark 11:13–14 there is a reference to a fig tree. This incident made such an impression upon the disciples that they drew the Lord's attention to it again in Mark 11:20. Then finally the Lord said, 'From the fig tree learn its lesson.' (Mark 13:28). We have to ask ourselves therefore whether these references to the fig tree have to be understood in relation to one another.

On the morning of the first day, the disciples saw that the Lord was hungry. They watched him go over to a fig tree and look for fruit, when he knew perfectly well that there could not be fruit on it at that time of the year. Mark draws our attention to this fact in Mark 11:13. In other words, Jesus was using this fig tree as an object lesson or as an 'acted' parable. After pronouncing a word of judgment on the tree, he went into the temple and with a scourge drove out all who had made it a place of commerce and cheating saying, 'Is it not written, "My house shall be called a house of prayer for all the nations"? But you have made it a den of robbers' (Mark 11:15–18, Revised Standard Version).

The next morning the disciples saw that the fig tree had withered from its roots and Peter drew the Lord's attention to it (Mark 11:20, 21). It is instructive to note that it was not a blight which had killed the fig tree. It had died from its roots. The end of Mark 11 and all of chapter 12 goes on to describe the final confrontation between the Messiah and the Jewish people. It must be understood that this confrontation was not with the vast majority of the people but with the leadership. The leaders of the various parties came with their trick questions. Their deliberate intention was to trap him, but they failed. The Messiah had come officially to the temple to look for fruit but he had found only leaves. It is Matthew who gives the fullest account of this confrontation and records that it ended with the severest denunciation ever recorded in Scripture (Matthew 23:37). That solemn message ended with those heart searing words 'O Jerusalem, Jerusalem, who kills the prophets and stones those who are sent to her! How often I wanted to gather your children together, the way a hen gathers her chicks under her wings and you were unwilling. Behold your house is being left to you desolate' (New American Standard Bible).

It would have been a terrible thing if these had been the final words of our Lord to the Jewish people but they were not. This is where so many Christian preachers have made their mistake. They have pronounced final judgment on the Jewish people as though these were the last words the Messiah had uttered, giving no hope or future to the Jew whatsoever. The concluding words of our Lord however, were not, 'your house is being left to you desolate,' or 'from now on you shall not see me.' There was a glorious 'until.' 'for I say to you, from now on you shall not see me until you say, "Blessed is he who comes in the name of the Lord."' These words, 'Welcome in the name of the Lord,' are the traditional and age-old Hebrew greeting 'Baruch haba ba shem Adonai.' In modern Hebrew if we want to say welcome we say 'Baruch Haba'. Literally it means 'blessed is he who comes'. The rejected Messiah was saying that there would come a day when the nation who had rejected him would receive him.

As the Messiah was leaving the temple for the last time, the disciples drew his attention to the magnificent stones of the temple and he told them that not one of those stones would be left on another. The fig tree would wither from its roots. It was not a blight from without to within, but an inner withering from its roots. It was an evil heart of unbelief which resulted in judgment. Passing out through the gates Jesus and his disciples descended into the Kidron valley, crossed the brook and climbed to some point on the Mount of Olives. Later on that day and somewhere on the mount overlooking the temple and city, a few of the disciples came privately and asked Christ, 'When will the temple be destroyed, and these stones cast down so that there is not one left upon another? What will be the sign of your return and of the end of the world?' He touched on a number of matters that would characterize the end and then said, 'From the fig tree learn its lesson' (Mark 13:28, Revised Standard Version).

It is an inescapable conclusion that the events connected with the fig tree during the previous two days must be related to what the Lord said here. If they are not, then it seems unfortunate to say the least, that the fig tree was used as an illustration at all. Its use would be misleading and certainly open to misinterpretation. Since the Spirit of truth has carefully inspired and governed the writing of the Scriptures it is much more likely that these incidents concerning the fig tree are related. Christ had used that fig tree as an object lesson and as an acted parable and was now drawing their attention to this.

Surely in this statement Jesus was gathering up all that the fig tree represents in the Bible as a symbol of the people of God. I know that some would say that the parable of the fig tree has nothing to do with the Jewish people but is to be understood only as a picture of spring pointing to coming summer. They quote Luke 21:29 in support of this view: 'Behold the fig tree and *all the trees*.' They feel that Christ used the fig tree as an illustration because it was one of the most common fruit trees to be found in Israel at that time. From nature therefore, he illustrated the way in which we know that winter has ended and summer is approaching. They would say that the lesson is simply that when we see the things he has told us about coming to pass, we know that his coming is near. The destruction of the temple and of Jerusalem in Seventy A.D. appears to support this view. At that stage in history there seemed no possibility of the Jewish people regaining their sovereignty and independence. In fact quite the opposite took place and Seventy A.D. marked the end of their nationhood and the dispersal of the nation throughout the world.

Since the fig tree has so many associations with the covenant people of God, why did Jesus refer to it? Why did he not take some other common fruit tree such as the almond or the pomegranate, both of them with symbolic significance? If he had used the almond tree as an illustration of coming summer, it would have been perfect. The almond is the first tree to flower in Israel and is the true harbinger of spring. Furthermore it is a symbol in the Old Testament of resurrection life and of spring after winter. Even the pomegranate would have been a good choice, symbolizing the fruitfulness of summer. Or why did he not simply say, 'When you see all the trees . . . ?' It would have been quite as good an illustration and without any possibility of mis-interpretation. It appears to me that Luke here is emphasizing this *particular* tree and that far from implying merely that summer was coming, he focuses our attention on that one par-ticular tree, namely the fig tree.

The fig tree along with the vine and olive tree, had often been used as a symbol in the Old Testament. It had been used firstly as a symbol of the Promised land itself, of its plentiful abundance and fertility and of the possession of it (e.g. Deuteronomy 8:8, 1 Kings 4:25, 2 Kings 18:31, Haggai 2:19, and Zechariah 3:10). Secondly, it was used as a symbol of the covenant people of God and their fruitfulness (e.g. Joel 1:7, Hosea 9:10; cf. Luke 13:6–9). By New Testament times therefore, the fig tree had associations in the popular mind with the land and the people of God, with both the nation and its national territory. The way in which the Lord Jesus used the fig tree in the parable recorded in Luke 13:6–9 is surely conclusive evidence that he associated the fig tree with the Jewish people. For the three years of his public ministry he had looked for fruit and found none. The 'acted' parable of Mark 11 must be seen in this light.

It therefore seems reasonably clear that in the parable of the fig tree we have a reference to the Jewish people — an infinitely gracious intimation that towards the end of the age something will happen to the judged, dispersed and despised

Jewish people. Christ said in Mark 13:28, 'From the fig tree learn its lesson: as soon as its branch becomes tender and puts forth its leaves, you know that summer is near' (Revised Standard Version). Surely he meant by this that this judged people, this people who were to wither from their roots, would still be there at the end of the age. They would in fact 'put forth leaves again.' Though dispersed to the ends of the earth, they would eventually come back to the land and would be reconstituted as a nation. If they were judged because of their fruitlessness, do we not find here the promise of final fruitfulness?

Thus the initial lesson of the fig tree is that when we see the events which Christ predicted being fulfilled, we shall know that his coming is at hand. As surely as summer follows spring and the trees bursting into leaf herald the coming of summer, so will the coming of Christ follow the events predicted in Matthew 24 and Mark 13. The deeper lesson of the fig tree is that towards the end something will happen to the rejected and dispersed Jewish people and this too will be an unmistakably clear indication that his coming is near. It is not just a question of all the trees breaking into leaf, although at no time in history has there been the birth of so many new nations as in the last thirty years. There is a particular tree among the trees to which our attention is drawn – the fig tree.

In this deeper sense, the parable of the fig tree has a three-fold significance. It speaks firstly of the continuity of the Jewish people. In spite of those sombre words of Christ, 'your house is left unto you desolate' (Matthew 23:38) and the even more awesome words of the people, 'his blood be on us and on our children' (Matthew 27:25), which led to the destruction of the temple and of Jerusalem, the break-up and dispersion of the Jewish nation to the ends of the earth and the beginning of nineteen hundred years of persecution, hatred and bloodshed; in spite of all this, after centuries of exiled misery, Israel would still be there at the close of the age. The fig tree would be there as a sign.

The survival of the Jewish people throughout their long history of suffering and dispersion is unparalleled in the annals of time except by the survival of the true Church of God. Many other peoples much more famous in their day, more established and more powerful than the Jews, have long since been absorbed by other nations. Today it is impossible to identify people like the Babylonians and the Assyrians. They have disappeared without facing anything like the persecution which the Jews have faced through their long and anguished history. Wherever Jews have settled in the world, they have adopted the language of the various peoples amongst whom they have lived and to a certain extent absorbed their culture. There is a vast difference superficially between a Yemenite or Moroccan Jew and an American or British Jew. Even so they have never been fully assimilated by those cultures and have remained essentially one distinct people. The survival of the Jewish people is a sign to the nations that God directs and governs history. At the end of the age the fig tree is still there.

We ought to pay attention to the Lord's words, 'Verily I say unto you, that this generation shall not pass away till all these things be done' (Mark 13:30, Authorized version). There are three possible interpretations of this statement. The first interpretation is that the Lord meant by 'this generation' that those who were actually listening to him would not die till all those matters of which he had been speaking were fulfilled. The problem with this view is that a number of the events which Christ predicted were not fulfilled within that period and others appear to have been only partially fulfilled. Those who do not believe in the full authority and inspiration of the Bible answer this objection by saying that Jesus was limited by his humanity and believed that within that generation, everything including his own return, would come to pass. The second interpretation is that 'this generation' refers to a future generation which would witness the fig tree blossoming. The generation which would witness the events Christ predicted beginning to be fulfilled, in particular, the re-creation of the state of Israel, would not pass away till all the rest were fulfilled. The only problem here is that it would have been much more correct for our Lord to have said 'that generation shall not pass away' whereas in fact He said 'this generation'. The third interpretation is that he meant by 'this generation', the Jewish people and their continuity. Those who hold this view point out that the Greek word translated here 'generation' can and should be translated by the English word 'race'. (See New American Standard Bible margin.) They would make the verse refer to the continuity of the Jewish people throughout the whole age — 'this race shall not pass away . . .'. It is true that the original Greek word had a rather indefinite and generalized meaning. Primarily it meant a begetting, rather than that which is begotten; a family and thus a generation, that is people born at the same time. The word then came to denote the time or period in which those people lived, approximately a period of thirty or forty years. It also had the wider meaning of a race of people born of the same origin and possessing the same characteristics.

It seems that all three interpretations are in fact valid and are covered by the way in which our Lord spoke. It may well be that he used this word ambiguously to cover these various ideas. The destruction of Jerusalem and the dispersion of the Jewish people to the ends of the earth, did in fact take place within that generation. It was in Seventy A.D. that Jerusalem and the temple were finally destroyed and the nation ceased to exist as a national entity. That same generation which heard our Lord's words began to see the fulfilment of those things he had predicted. Secondly, it could mean that the generation which witnesses the re-creation of the state of Israel will in fact see the fulfilment of all the other events. Thirdly, underlying both of these and probably the most significant, the Jewish people though judged, though dispersed, though losing their national entity, their national territory and the physical centre of their religious life, the temple and the priesthood, would still be there at the end of the age. They would have survived all the hatred of the nations into which they were dispersed. Christ predicted that they would survive whatever should come against them be it persecution , or pogroms,*or the Nazi holocaust of 1939–1945, in which six million Jews were to die, or every other threat made against them. Thus first and foremost the parable of the fig tree speaks of the continuity of the Jewish people.

Secondly, the parable of the fig tree speaks of the reconstitution of the Jewish nation and the repossession of its national territory. The fig tree cursed and withered portrays the nation rejected and dispersed; the fig tree putting forth its leaves again portrays the nation reconstituted and the land regained. The Jewish people would not lose their racial or religious identity or their national consciousness, but they would lose their nationhood and their land. Although the nation would be utterly broken up and cease to function as a nation, yet at the end it would again come into its own. This

*See appendix.

would be in spite of nineteen hundred years of lost national sovereignty.

The re-creation of the state of Israel in 1948 against all odds was a miracle. It was the fulfilment of that which God had spoken through his prophets. For example, the Lord says in Isaiah 43:5 'Fear not for I am with thee, I will bring thy seed from the East and gather thee from the West. I will say to the North, Give up and to the South, Keep not back. Bring my sons from far, and my daughters from the end of the earth.' We know that this has a very real spiritual meaning, but it also has a physical or literal fulfilment. We are told by some that these words of the prophet Isaiah were fulfilled in the return from Babylon, but they did not at that time come from the South and from the West, they only came from the North and from the East. When has Israel been gathered from East and West and from North and South, indeed from the ends of the earth? Although at the turn of the century Jews began to return again to the land, it has only been since 1948 and during the subsequent years that this prophecy has been literally fulfilled. They have returned from the ends of the earth. In these years there has been a most remarkable fulfilment of this word. Even the statement – 'I will say to the North, Give up', has a contemporary ring, for who would have thought that the vast monolithic giant, the Soviet Union would ever let any of its citizens emigrate? Yet the Kremlin has had to let go thousands of the three million Jews that are resident within the Soviet Union. I believe that because of God's word, they will have to let many more thousands go.

Another example of prophecy being fulfilled is in Isaiah 61:4–5, 'and they shall build the old wastes, they shall raise up the former desolations, they shall repair the waste cities, the desolations of many generations and strangers shall stand and feed your flocks and foreigners shall be your ploughmen and your vine dressers.' One has to ask when this word was literally fulfilled? Again some would tell us that its fulfilment was in the return from Babylon. There is no doubt that there was at that time a partial fulfilment of these words, but the word of God says 'they shall repair the waste cities, the desolations of *many generations*.' In the return from Babylon the desolations then, were of one or at the most of two generations. The captivity lasted seventy years and the exile lasted forty or maybe fifty years, but it consisted of no more than two generations. It has only been in this century that city after city in Israel has been built upon the old wastes, the desolations of many generations. Arad, Ashdod, Ashkelon and Beer-sheba are but four examples. Furthermore, there has never been a time when so many non-Jewish people have been wanting to help in the rebuilding of the land and the recovery of its fruitfulness. The Jewish Agency has lists of young Gentile men and women who want to work in kibbutzim in Israel. Some of them already there are feeding the flocks and being ploughmen and vine dressers. Another example is in Amos 9:14–15. 'and I will bring back the captivity of my people Israel and they shall build the waste cities and inhabit them, they shall plant vineyards and drink the wine thereof, they shall also make gardens and eat the fruit of them and I will plant them upon their land and they shall no more be plucked up out of their land which I have given them, saith the Lord thy God.' To say as many do, that this was fulfilled in the return from Babylon is to make God if not a liar, certainly an exaggerator, for God said, 'I will plant them upon their land and they shall no more be plucked up out of their land which I have given them.' To say that the Lord was referring to the return from Babylon, is to make out that he was ignoring the greatest dispersion in Jewish history which took place in Seventy A.D. and has lasted one thousand nine hundred years until this century. The fact is, that the fulfilment of these words has taken place in our own generation. It has been within this generation that they have built the waste cities and inhabited them, that they have planted vineyards on what were arid barren hills and have created fruitful gardens as anyone can see who has visited the kibbutzim and moshavim of Israel. Another example is in Zephaniah 2:4–7 where the prophet Zephaniah says 'For Gaza shall be forsaken and Ashkelon a desolation; they shall drive out Ashdod at noonday and Ekron shall be rooted up. Woe unto the inhabitants of the sea-coast, the nation of the Cherethites! The word of the Lord is against you, O Canaan, the land of the Philistines; I will destroy thee, that there shall be no inhabitant. And the sea-coast shall be pastures, with cottages for shepherds and folds for flocks. And the coast shall be for the remnant of the house of Judah; they shall feed their flocks thereupon; in the houses of Ashkelon shall they lie down in the evening; for the Lord their God will visit them and bring back their captivity.' When the children of God returned from Babylon they certainly did not possess Gaza, Ashdod, Ashkelon or Ekron. Indeed Ashkelon, where it is believed by some that Herod the Great was born, was a city that most good Jews abhorred. It was almost totally Gentile in its outlook and atmosphere. These words were not even fulfilled in 1948 but in 1957 when with funds from South African Jewry, the city of Ashkelon was once again built upon the desolation of many generations. It is moving to see in the town square of this rebuilt Ashkelon these words of the prophet Zephaniah in Hebrew inscribed on stone. Since then the city of Ashdod has also been rebuilt and is destined to become Israel's largest port and Gath, the city which so many Christians associate with the Philistines, has become a thriving newly built Jewish city, and the centre of the Israeli textile industry.

Indeed this whole passage is remarkable, for it is quite contemporary. The Lord said 'The word of the Lord is against you O Canaan, the land of the Philistines.' In Hebrew the word for Philistine is Pilishtim, and in modern Arabic the Palestinian calls himself a Falastin. Then we get the word Jew from Judah. So here we make a remarkable discovery; we have the Palestinian leaving and we have the Jew coming in.

Some may well feel as they read this that I find no place in the economy of God for the Arab peoples but this is not true. I believe firmly that the purpose of God for the Arab peoples is their salvation and not their subjugation or exploitation. No people have been more cynically exploited than the Arab poor, not least by their own pashas (lords) and big landowners. The question is how that purpose of God to save the Arab peoples could be fulfilled. I believe it will be through Israel, for if God's purpose is to make her the means of blessing to all the nations, the Arabs will be no exception. For the Arabs to fight against Israel is for them to fight against God and their own blessing and well-being. Indeed, every time the Arab nations or the Palestinians have fought against Israel, generally with the odds very much on their side, they have lost not only the war but more territory. The acceptance of the state of Israel by the Arab peoples both within and without Israel's borders would lead inevitably to peace not war, to enrichment not exploitation, to blessing not colonization and slavery. It would lead to the fulfilment of such scriptures as Isaiah 19:23–25. The tragedy is that in general the Arabs fail to see this and even more sadly the Christian Arabs. One cannot help but feel that the Lebanon story would have been different if the Lebanese Arab Christians had only understood this from the beginning. There could have been a mutual enrichment and security as in the days of Solomon, King of Israel and Hiram, King of Tyre.*

To those who tell me that the Jew has no future but is rejected by God and under his judgment and curse, let me ask only this one question, Why does Satan hate these people so much? One would have thought that if they had done the devil's work, as some would have us believe, he would surely have left them alone. The opposite however, has been the case. For just as Satan put it into the heart of Herod to kill all the children in Bethlehem in order to destroy the Messiah and prevent the purpose of God being fulfilled, so Satan put it into the heart of Hitler to destroy the Jewish people in order to prevent the re-creation of the state of Israel. If many Christians do not recognize the significance of the Jewish people, of their survival and of the re-creation of the state of Israel, the powers of darkness certainly do. Nevertheless, just as God time and again has turned the work of Satan to good account and has used it to fulfil his purpose, so he made Adolf Hitler, Heinrich Himmler, Adolf Eichmann and the other Nazi henchmen, the dynamic for the reconstitution of the state of Israel.

When Theodor Herzl went throughout Europe and elsewhere at the end of the nineteenth century warning of coming persecution and pleading with the leaders of Jewry to support a Jewish national state, apart from some noble exceptions, his views were greeted with derision. In some instances Jewish leaders said that they were more German than the Germans. It is no wonder that many of his close friends felt that his death at an early age [in his forties] was due mainly to a broken heart. Yet God undoubtedly raised him up to be the pioneer of Zionism and through him fulfilled his prophetic purpose. Although he was not orthodox in his religious belief, much of what he said was prophetic in content. After the first Zionist Congress in Basle in 1897, he wrote in his diary, 'At Basle I founded the Jewish state. If I were to say this today, I would be greeted with laughter. In

*See appendix, 'The Dilemma For The Palestinian'.

five years perhaps and certainly in fifty, everyone will see it.'
It would seem that he had some sense of divine mission.
When he was dying, he called for one of his close friends, a
Jewish Christian who was chaplain to the British Embassy in
Vienna and one of the speakers at the first Zionist Congress.
Theodor Herzl divulged to this friend that when he was twelve
years of age he had had a dream in which he had seen a man
who appeared very old but full of majesty and who had said
to him, 'I have raised you up that you might be the means of
bringing my people together again from the ends of the earth.'
Although he did not live to see such things come to pass,
Theodor Herzl is now universally recognized as the founder
of the state of Israel and his body now lies not in Europe
where he died but in Jerusalem.

However it was the Nazi era that provided the overwhelming impetus for the creation of a Jewish state. When at the end
of the holocaust there were two million Jewish survivors, half
of whom were under the age of twelve, no one wanted them.
Neither the nations of Western Europe nor the nations of
Eastern Europe wanted them. Even America and Canada
were not open to receive them. For example, in 1946 the
United States Congress would only allow a mere 4,760
Jewish refugees to enter. So the unfortunate Jewish survivors
of the concentration camps and the Second World War were
once again housed in the very same camps in which they had
seen a third of their people destroyed. It is true that the
concentration camps had been cleaned up and that there was
proper food, and medical care provided. Yet for those
survivors it was a time of horror that having come as a people
to the brink of total annihilation and having survived, no one
wanted them. It was the realization of this fact that fanned in
the hearts of these survivors the original vision of Theodor
Herzl. They realized that unless the Jewish people had their
own state, they would never be safe again, nor would they
ever be able to lift their heads high in a world that hated them.
Thus the wickedness of Hitler and his henchmen and the
latent anti-semitism in the world became the means of the
creation of the state of Israel. For thousands upon thousands
of these people, both young and old, were drawn by some
unseen magnetic force back to the land of their forefathers.
They began the trek across Europe, over the Alps and down
to the Mediterranean ports to embark upon any vessel which

floated, to take them there.

Even the might of Britain could not stop them. The British Government decided not only to restrict Jews immigrating into Palestine by interning them in Cyprus, but to forcibly return to the former concentration camps in Germany thousands of those who had run the blockade aboard such ships as 'The Exodus'. This only furthered the resolve of the Jewish people to settle in Palestine no matter what the cost. In the end the British found the problem too great and asked the United Nations to take over the mandate. The U.N. faced a complex problem. The General Assembly required a two thirds majority to pass any resolution. The Arabs refused to countenance any other recommendation than that all of Palestine should be declared an Arab state. They warned that anything else would lead to war. To offset the vote of the Muslim nations alone required one third of the votes of the General Assembly. The British Government said that they would only co-operate with any partition plan if both the Arabs and the Jews were enthusiastic partners, a contingency they knew to be impossible. Then there was the heated problem of Jerusalem. Both Jews and Arabs demanded sovereignty over the city, while many other states, including the Vatican, demanded internationalization. For the Jews, a state without Jerusalem was a contradiction in terms. Humanly speaking, the odds were heavily against the creation of a Jewish state. The Soviet bloc was against the proposal to begin with, while many other nations vacillated. It was in fact, President Truman who unexpectedly threw his personal weight behind the proposal for partition that made a significant difference. The historic decision by the U.N. General Assembly in November, 1947, to partition Palestine was passed by a vote of 33 in favour, 13 against and 10 abstentions. Thus the U.N. gave to the Jewish people, a Jewish state. It was but further evidence that God determines the course of history, for it was against all odds. The fig tree had again put forth her leaves.

We all give verbal assent to the power of prayer, but how many of us really believe that it is prayer that can determine the course of history? Any Christian who knows the story of Rees Howells and those who prayed with him in Swansea during the years of the Second World War must surely realize how much their prayer determined the course of the war and the final overthrow of Nazism. One great prayer burden continuing throughout those war years was for the Jewish people. The burden was that despite Hitler's attempts to liquidate them, they would be safeguarded and that they would return to Palestine and establish a Jewish state. Rees Howells saw this to be the will of God from the Scriptures. As early as September, 1938, with the proclamation by Italy that all Jews there must leave within six months, continual prayer was made by Rees Howells and those with him. However, it was after the war in October and November of 1947, that whole days were given to prayer. On eleven different days during those two months, prayer was concentrated on the coming U.N. vote. When on November 27th, the news came through that the partition of Palestine had not been carried, the whole Bible College, of which Rees Howells was the founder and principal, gave themselves to intense intercession. In prayer they actually became aware of God's angels influencing the men in the U.N. debate. Before hearing the final outcome they already had full assurance of victory. When on November 29th the news came that the partition proposal had been carried, the College claimed it as one of the greatest days for God in 1900 years! Moreover it was the Soviet Union and Soviet bloc which reversed its attitude and cast the deciding votes in favour of partition. In the light of present history, what further evidence could there be of the truth of God's word as spoken through the psalmist, 'even the wrath of men shall praise thee.' (Psalm 76:10)? A Jewish state had become reality. The fact is that this scattered people was regathered by some sovereign and irresistible power and reconstituted as a nation among the nations. They were brought back to the very territory from which they had been uprooted, to regain their nationhood and their national sovereignty.

It was not only the creation of the Jewish state that was a miracle but its survival. In 1948 its population numbered 650,000 and it faced five regular Arab armies, all fully mobilized and actively aided by one million Palestinian Arabs. Israel faced that colossal onslaught with a few thousand rifles, a few hundred machine guns, an assortment of other fire-arms, not a single cannon or tank and nine aeroplanes, only one of them with two engines! Of those 650,000 men and women, only 48,000 were trained in any

elimentary way to fight. Yet they not only survived, they
triumphed and it was God's doing. The story of miraculous
deliverance and triumph has continued throughout Israel's
twenty-eight years of history. (cf. Luke 21:24, 'until'.)

It was not only national territory and national sovereignty
that was regained but the national language that was restored.
Hebrew for thousands of years a sacred but dead language,
has now become the spoken living language of a virile nation.
This again is the fulfilment of the prophetic word. Jeremiah
the prophet said in Jeremiah 31:23, 'Thus saith the Lord of
hosts, the God of Israel, yet again shall they use this speech in
the land of Judah and in the cities thereof, when I shall bring
again their captivity'. The reconstitution of Hebrew as a living
national language is one of the miracles of our day. It was not
the product of a college of professors or a movement of
academics, but was principally the work of one man, Eliezer
ben Yehuda. Eliezer ben Yehuda 'lived', 'slept' and 'ate'
Hebrew. At the beginning he was thought to be a crazy
eccentric, but he was in fact, a man of vision. He believed that
unless the Jewish people spoke one language they would be
hopelessly divided by a babel of tongues. Such was his
passion that he would not allow any word to be spoken to his
children other than Hebrew. Eliezer ben Yehuda was one of
those unique figures who lived to see the fulfilment of his
vision. Before he died in 1922, he was to hear melodious
Hebrew spoken by a young generation of Israeli Sabras. It is
amazing to consider that so much depended on the work of
this one man. Sometimes the research required to discover
one Hebrew word for a modern idea would take four or five
years and in some cases ten years. Whenever new information
came to him about a word he would write it down on a little
scrap of paper. His study was full of mounds of these small
pieces of paper. His wife could only get him to tidy it up by
telling him that the mice were eating the Hebrew language!
On one occasion he lost a particular word that had taken
years of research and the whole house was turned upside
down with everybody looking for this little piece of paper
until it was found finally in the turnup of his own trousers.
There is no other record of a modern language being spoken
in the world today which having ceased to exist as a spoken
language for thousands of years has then been revived. There
is a great and justifiable battle over Welsh and Irish for

example, but these have never ceased to be spoken. The battle is for their survival and full acceptance. Hebrew however, ceased to be a spoken language of the Jewish home and of the community for some two thousand years. It was only a sacred and liturgical language. The miracle is that it has once again become the spoken language of Parliament, of the universities, of commerce, of the street and of the home. It is the language of radio and television. Newspapers, magazines and books are all published in Hebrew. The words of Jeremiah have been literally fulfilled. If Jeremiah were now to stand in the streets of Tel Aviv or Jerusalem he would understand the present day speech much more than that of the people in the days of our Lord when Aramaic, a sister language to Hebrew, was spoken. In all these matters we see that the fig tree has put forth its leaves again.

Thirdly, the parable of the fig tree must speak of fruitfulness. The fig tree was cursed because it was barren. Surely the reference to the fig tree bursting into leaf must mean that through the grace and power of God alone, the Jewish people will finally bear fruit unto God. Truly believing in the Messiah, they will once more be brought back into the elect people of God. This does not of course mean the whole Israeli nation, or all Jews, any more than we understand 'all Gentiles' from the phrase 'the fulness of the Gentiles,' but it does mean the elect among them (see Romans 11:23–25).

It seems to me that there is no point in mentioning the fig tree as bursting into leaf unless it speaks of summer fruitfulness, especially when we consider it in the light of the earlier fig tree. That fig tree was cursed because it bore no fruit and consisted only of leaves. Surely this reference to the fig tree putting forth leaves again can only mean the promise of fruit. So we might well look for something even more wonderful and miraculous than the survival of the Jewish people or the reconstitution of the Jewish nation and the regaining by them of their national territory. There will be a tremendous ingathering of Jewish people to the Messiah. Then all Israel – the true Israel of God, the elect people of God gathered out of time – will be saved for his coming again.

11. My Heart's Desire

There rests upon every true Christian a solemn and inescapable responsibility towards Israel and the Jewish people. To be a true Christian, to be born of the Spirit of God and yet to be anti-Semitic or anti-Jewish is a contradiction in terms. There is not a single Christian who is not indebted to the Jewish people, for 'to them belong the sonship, the glory, the covenants, the giving of the law, the worship and the promises; to them belong the patriarchs and of their race, according to the flesh, is the Messiah' Romans 9:45, Revised Standard Version. Furthermore, it was Jewish lips and Jewish bodies that first brought the good news of the salvation of God to the Gentiles. In the midst of heated controversy, ignoring the derision heaped upon them, those early Jewish apostles set out to reach the whole world for the Messiah. For the sake of both Jew and Gentile they accepted 'the offence of the cross' and laid down their lives willingly that others might come to know and experience the saving power of God. There is no true believer in this world, whatever their colour may be or on whatever continent they may be found, whose experience of the love and grace of God cannot be traced back to those early Jewish believers. The early church was totally Jewish in its origin, its thinking and its background. Yet they saw their responsibility to take the Gospel to the Gentiles, no matter how great the cost, how fierce the conflict, or how painful the misunderstanding. If they had not brought the Gospel to the Gentiles, no Gentile would ever have been saved and those Christians who indulge in anti-Semitism would never have had the chance of knowing Christ.

Then again, we ought to consider the mysterious and profound statement clothed in such simple words 'by their fall salvation is come to the Gentiles.' (Romans 11:12). Whatever we might feel about this matter, the fact is that it was through the fall of the Jewish people that salvation came to the Gentile world. We should ponder deeply upon the Apostle's words. For he goes on to state that the fall and the loss of the Jewish people has become the very riches of the Gentile world; that their being cast away has spelt the glorious reality of reconciliation for a world alienated from God and his word. At the very least, through the fall of the Jewish people, the Mosaic law and the prophetic burden has become a worldwide possession. There is no corner of the earth that the moral law contained in the ten commandments has not reached, while for the vast majority of civilized nations it has become the basis for society. At the time the Mosaic law was given, it was unique among the nations. The basic concepts of marriage and of family life, of justice, of national righteousness, of hygiene, of the care of the poor, the widow and the orphan, and the supreme concept of the dignity and preciousness of human life are all contained within it. The burden of the prophets for national and social righteousness as well as for a living relationship to God and genuine spiritual values, maintained and underlined these truths. The fall of the Jewish people has meant that this priceless heritage, this revelation of God's heart and mind for man, has enriched the whole Gentile world. For the truth of God expressed in the Old and New Testaments has radically influenced the nations of the earth. Christians need to remember that there would have been no New Testament but for the Old Testament. The Gospel which is the flowering and the fulfilment of the Old Testament has changed society wherever it has come. Education for all, medical work, national righteousness and ethics, honest and uncorrupt government, an equitable judicial system, social welfare and prison reform have all followed in its wake. All this essential truth which the nations of the West are at present in danger of losing, came through the Jewish people, and has through their fall been disseminated to the ends of the earth.

That fall, that casting away and loss, has been written in one thousand nine hundred years of Jewish sorrow and anguish. What hideous interpretation of God's word can it be that has encouraged Christians to despise the Jew in his sorrow, to curse him and by every means possible to remind him that he is under divine judgement? The history of the institutional church, whatever name it bears, has deep stains in this matter, for terrible things have been done to the Jew in the name of Christ, ranging from the inquisition to pogroms on Good Friday.

Yet it was their fall that brought salvation to the Gentiles. If those who have experienced the grace of God and his salvation should love the whole world, how much more should they love that people by whose fall they have come to know God. The very fact of the thousands of years of their wandering exile, of the persecution that has driven them from place to place, of their being the offscouring of the world, should surely incite in the true Christian, the tenderest love towards them, since through their failure and loss, he has been saved. The anguished Jewish cry that rings down through the centuries of their bloodstained history ought then to find an echo in the heart of the true Christian and if it does not, it is a terrible condemnation.

Is it possible to love God and to hate or dislike those whom he loves? By divine inspiration Paul says 'but as regards election they are beloved for the sake of the forefathers'. This is rendered simply in the Living Bible as 'yet the Jews are still beloved of God because of his promises to Abraham, Isaac, and Jacob'. In the light of this it is surely impossible for the love of God to be shed abroad in our hearts and for there to be no place in them for the Jew. It is unthinkable that one could love and serve Christ the Messiah, whose glorified and risen body is Jewish according to the flesh and not love the people from whom he came. The nearer we live to God and to Christ, the more we shall feel something of God's eternal heart-beat for the Jewish people.

The Apostle Paul says in Romans 10:1, 'my heart's desire and prayer to God for Israel is that they might be saved.' We need a heart of love above all else in this matter. So often even those Christians who recognize God's purpose in the Jewish people and see the hand of God in the re-creation of the state of Israel, only look upon them as a kind of object lesson. Their heads and minds are involved in the marvellous fulfilment of prophecy but their hearts are not involved with that people. Yet the Lord seeks for those whose hearts can be so brought into tune with him, that his Spirit can produce a longing that will find relief only in costly prayer. This 'heart's desire and prayer to God for Israel' is no superficial matter. Paul speaks of having 'great sorrow and unceasing pain in his heart' for them. This is the missing note in the Christian's attitude to the Jewish people. It can of course, be argued that the Apostle was himself Jewish and therefore quite rightly and naturally had such longings for his own people. It is only right that everyone of us should desire the salvation of our own kith and kin, the people from whom we have sprung. I cannot help however but believe that this desire in Paul's heart went deeper than that, for he beyond all others saw more clearly the purpose of God for the Jewish people. In Romans 9–11 and in other passages he wrestles with human language to explain and interpret what he has seen. So vast is the subject, so mysterious the purpose of God, that at times he appears almost to contradict himself. Even with divine inspiration, human language cannot fully convey the truth. What he does make abundantly clear is that God desires to save Israel, not throw her away. That desire of God has somehow overflowed into Paul's own heart and given rise in him to costly prayer.

We have therefore, to ask ourselves whether it is possible to be saved by the grace of God, to love him truly and not share the desire that is in his heart? Could it be possible to live in fellowship with the Lord Jesus and serve him from a pure heart and despise or even hate the people from whom, according to the flesh, he came? It is certainly not possible and there rests upon every true child of God a solemn responsibility not only to stand with Israel and the Jewish people, but to love them from a pure heart. Love such as this will lead to the kind of prayer that only the Holy Spirit can give, it will lead to importunate and travailing prayer. If every so-called Christian had been filled with the love of God, many phases of Jewish history might have been very different. It is therefore incumbent upon every true Christian to seek to redress the balance and eradicate forever the caricature of Christianity which has been presented to them. That balance can only be redressed by a heart of love.

Such love born out of a pure heart will lead not only to a sacrificial and consistent ministry of prayer for Israel, but also to a preparedness to be identified with Israel in her fight for life. If German Christians had only stood up when the first manifestos were issued from beer stalls in Southern Germany by Hitler in the early thirties, history might have been different. Instead the German Church was silent, until she became so compromised in the web of national politics and economics that she lost her soul. Some like Dietrich Bonhoeffer, did stand up and clear themselves at the cost of their lives, but this was too late and the vast majority of German Christians by their silence became partakers in Nazi sin. The same dilemma on a much wider scale faces the Christians of our day. The U.N. resolution condemning Zionism as 'racism' will finally end in the same way as Hitler's beer hall manifestos. The true Church of God must either compromise or speak up. If every Christian had the same heart's desire for Israel as the Apostle Paul and the same great sorrow and unceasing pain in his or her heart, there would be no possibility of compromise.

If it is God who stands behind the re-creation of the state of Israel and if it is his prophetic word which has been and is being fulfilled, I can do no other as his servant than stand with him whatever the cost. There may be problems about many of the details, but the principle is clear. If it is his heart's desire that Israel should be saved, then it must be mine also.

12. Israel Saved

The battle for Israel is no modern phenomenon. Her right to exist and her claim to destiny has always been contested. From the very beginning of her history the powers of darkness and evil have sought to destroy her from both without and within. Whether we look in the pages of the Old Testament or in the pages of Jewish history, we find the same story. For even when the Jewish people lost their national sovereignty and territory and were scattered to the four corners of the earth, the battle did not cease. We are witnessing in our generation the climax of that battle. It will not cease until the Lord Jesus returns.

The focal point of that battle as far as flesh and blood goes, is all to do with territory and boundaries, with national rights and national security. That however, is not the real focal point of the battle and never has been. For Israel represents spiritual realities and values. The Israel of old has left us with no great monuments such as the pyramids of ancient Egypt, or great works of art such as the Chinese have left us. Instead she has given us the word of God. In this we see her history set forth as a living, dynamic relationship with God. This lesson is seen both positively at the high points of her spiritual life and negatively during those times when she fell away from the Lord. God was teaching Israel that everything depends upon a right relationship to himself. It is in this way that the whole history of Israel is the setting forth of spiritual realities. It is not a matter of secular history but the unfolding of God's purpose to save mankind. Furthermore through the rejection of the Messiah and the fall of the Jewish people, the saving power of God has gone forth to the ends of the earth. From every corner of the world God has brought Gentiles to a saving knowledge of himself through Jesus the crucified Messiah. When the fulness of the Gentiles has been gathered in, then the hardness which has befallen Israel in part will be done away and all the true Israel of God will have been saved. For this reason the powers of darkness hate Israel and all that she represents of the sovereign purpose and power of God. In all that is happening over Israel and the Jewish people in our generation, we see the fulfilment of divine prophecy and the outworking of God's purpose. It is the hatred of these spiritual powers of evil against God's purpose which occasions the battle. It is only the understanding of this conflict in its spiritual dimension that explains the mysterious and continuous hatred towards Israel throughout history and until this day.

There is no fear about the outcome. Israel will not only survive, she will triumph. She will do so not because of native genius or wit, or because of military prowess, but because of the grace of God. Stage by stage the nations will come to see that Israel's survival is a divine miracle. For the purpose of God is to reveal through Israel and through the blind hatred against her on the part of others, that there are spiritual principles involved. Whatever happens in these future years and there will undoubtedly be more wars, the nations that come against Israel will be broken because of her, for God has said so. No matter what comes against Israel, even if the whole world unites against her, she will triumph and they will all be broken. There is more to Israel than flesh and blood.

Despite all the heated controversy over this matter, the arguments for or against Israel and the debate over the Palestinian issue, the fact is that the Jewish people have come home to stay. For whatever we might think or feel, they will never again be rooted up out of the land. God has given his word on this matter. He has not only stated that the Jewish people will remain in the land but that this precious and beloved land will witness the final events of human history. All the great miracles of the end time will take place within her borders. This will surely be a most remarkable coincidence if as some say, God has finished with the Jewish people, and the re-creation of the state of Israel is a political accident and has nothing to do with him. It must be significant that all the major miraculous events to do with the last phase of world history will take place within Israel. That land will witness war and more war, but there will always be the miracle of Israeli survival and triumph. It will witness the whole northern military confederacy miraculously destroyed upon its mountains in a moment of time. It will witness the veil being taken away by God from the Jewish heart so that there will be national mourning over the death of Jesus and glorious salvation as a result. Finally it will witness that greatest of all miracles, the coming again of the Messiah. Zechariah prophesied that 'his feet shall stand in that day upon the Mount of Olives' (Zechariah 14:4).

Those blessed and pierced feet will once again touch the dust of the Mount of Olives. It is noteworthy that the Messiah does not return to the great capitals of the world. He does not come to Washington, to London, to Paris, to Moscow or to Peking. He does not come even to Rome with all its Christian associations, or to Geneva. He returns to Jerusalem. This must be a problem to those who do not see the hand of God in the re-creation of the state of Israel and in Jerusalem, its capital. In this city he was rejected, he was crucified and he rose again. From this city he ascended into heaven and to this city he will return. This was the place where he commissioned those Jewish apostles to go to every part of the world and proclaim the good news to every creature. It was here that the Jewish people fell and through that fall salvation came to the Gentiles. It was from Jerusalem that they were dispersed in Seventy A.D. throughout the whole world and it is to Jerusalem that they have now returned. It is the 'inhabitants of Jerusalem who when the spirit of grace and supplication is poured upon them, will lead the nation in looking unto him whom they have pierced'. (Zechariah 12:10). It is from their lips that he will hear those wonderful words of welcome, 'Blessed be he that comes in the name of the Lord'. With the return of the Messiah, the circle will be completed. All human history and Jewish history in particular will have found its fulfilment.

To me the person of Jesus is the master key to Jewish history. He is the Key of David. I believe that he is the Messiah because I can find no other adequate explanation for the one thousand and nine hundred years of Jewish exile. The only other instance of an exile was the seventy years of Babylonian captivity and that was due to the disobedience and idolatry of the people of God. One may well ask what could have occasioned one thousand and nine hundred years of exile and suffering but the rejection of the Messiah. This interprets for me the otherwise inexplicable course of the Jewish people since the events of Christ's birth, death and resurrection.

The battle for Israel of which we are witnesses will continue until the end of this age. For we are told that it will be only in the final battle when Israel will be overrun and half of Jerusalem will be taken captive, that the feet of the Messiah will stand again upon the Mount of Olives and the battle for Israel will have been won forever. Then Jewish history will be finally completed and all will recognize that at its heart lies the mystery and wonder of divine election.

How can we explain this mystery of divine election? It can only be explained as the tenacity of divine and infinite love. 'As concerning the gospel, they are enemies for your sakes: but as touching the election, they are beloved for the fathers' sakes' (Romans 11:28, Authorized Version). They became enemies because of God's love for the Gentiles, but are beloved because of their origin. It is precisely in relation to the Jewish people, that God's word declares that 'the gifts and the call of God are irrevocable' (Romans 11:29 Revised Standard Version). There are few instances in the whole history of God's dealings with men where his faithfulness, his love and his mercy shine more radiantly than here, or where the declaration of that love — 'He will not fail thee, nor forsake thee' (Deuteronomy 31:6) — is more amply demonstrated.

Can we ever explain God's love for Jacob? Can we ever explain God's love for us? Such love must surely baffle us. 'Jacob' means literally 'one who follows at the heel' and was used figuratively for one who supplants, circumvents, or deceives (see Genesis 25:31–26.) and Jacob lived up to his name. He stole his twin brother Esau's birthright and blessing, deceived his old father Isaac and swindled his uncle Laban, only to meet his match in him. Yet it was the grace of God which triumphed in Jacob.

To him came a revelation of God which was to change not only his name but also his character. The Lord wrestled with him all night and touched him at the heart of his being. 'Thy name shall be called no more Jacob, but Israel' (see Genesis 32:22–32). One interpretation for the name Israel is that it means 'God persists' or 'God perseveres'. It is certainly true that Jacob would never have become Israel but for the perseverance of God. Forever after it was that name Israel, with all its glorious meaning and significance, which was to be used for the elect people of God. At the very heart of their existence and of their salvation lies the faithful perseverance and persistence of God himself. This is the only explanation for the continuity and survival of the Jewish people, their reconstitution as a nation and their final ingathering to Jesus the Messiah.

In this way the words spoken concerning the Lord Jesus by that old and godly Jew, Simeon, will be fulfilled. That day in the temple, taking up the newly circumcized babe in his arms, he blessed him, praised God and said, 'for mine eyes have seen thy salvation, which thou hast prepared before the face of all people; a light to lighten the Gentiles and the glory of thy people Israel' (Luke 2:30–32 Authorized Version). In these wonderful words of Simeon the whole plan of God is encompassed. He condenses into a profound statement of one sentence the whole theme of the Bible. It explains not only the past and the present but also the future.

By the spirit of God Simeon said, 'mine eyes have seen thy salvation, which thou hast prepared before the face of all people.' From the beginning, the salvation of God was always intended for the whole world and the Jewish people were chosen by God to be the vehicle for that salvation. The Messiah came from that stock to be the Saviour of the world. From the promise of the 'seed of the woman' who would crush the serpent's head, (Genesis 3:15) down through the centuries of Old Testament history to the words of Malachi, 'the Lord will suddenly appear in his temple' (Malachi 3:1) and the cry of John the Baptist 'Prepare ye the way of the Lord' (Matthew 3:3) God had been working towards the coming of the Saviour. He had prepared his salvation before the face of all nations.

Simeon also went on to say of Jesus that he was 'a light to lighten the Gentiles.' God's plan that the Jewish people should become the means by which his light should shine to the end of the earth had its fulfilment in the Messiah. He could truly say, 'I am the light of the world. He that followeth me shall not walk in darkness but shall have the light of life.' (John 8:12). Even their rejection of the Messiah, has in the sovereignty of God, been turned into salvation and blessing for the Gentiles. From every tribe and tongue, from every people and nation, Gentiles have come to God. All the ends of the earth have seen his salvation. (Psalm 98:3).

Simeon concluded by calling the Lord Jesus 'the glory of thy people Israel'. The Messiah is the supreme glory of the Jewish people. At present they do not recognize him as their true glory, but in the end they will see him as the fulfilment of their history and the meaning of their destiny. When the fulness of the Gentiles has come in, then the veil will be taken away from the heart of the Jewish people and they will be grafted back. The Lord himself is the incomparable glory of the people of God and only his faithful persistence could have brought them into that glory.

Even more amazing is the fact that the Lord describes his people as 'Israel, my glory' (Isaiah 46:13). In the end the Lord will rejoice with joy unspeakable over a completed work. The ransomed will have returned to Zion and with them an innumerable multitude of those redeemed from the nations. Those Gentiles who were once afar off will have been brought near by the blood of the Messiah. At one time separate from the Messiah, excluded from the commonwealth of Israel and strangers to the covenants of promise, they will have been made fellow heirs, fellow members of the Body and fellow partakers of the promise in the Messiah Jesus. (Ephesians 2:12, 13; 3:6). The Lord Jesus shall have seen of the travail of his soul and be fully satisfied. He will exult over Israel with joy.

The Lord calls Israel his glory because only he could change a Jacob into an Israel. Such a statement can only be explained by his matchless grace. When all has been said that could be said, such grace and love, patient, steadfast, tireless and undying, are the only explanation for those glorious words: 'and so all Israel shall be saved' (Romans 11:26).

Appendix

1. ZIONISM

Zion originally was one of the mountains of Jerusalem, but it very quickly came to be another name for Jerusalem itself. For example in the Psalms of David, Jerusalem is often referred to as Zion. Furthermore, in both Jewish and Christian thought, Zion has come to represent a spiritual ideal. For most Jews today, to talk about Zionism is to talk about the return to the land and the re-creation and re-building of the Jewish state. For such Zionism is the embodiment of an ideal, both spiritual and practical.

Such aspirations have been present in many Jewish hearts throughout their two thousand years of exile and have led certain groups at various times to return to the land of Israel. However it was towards the end of the nineteenth century that a movement sprang up, both simultaneously and spontaneously in various parts of Europe, a movement within Jewry that eventually led them not only to return to the land in a manner and on a scale previously unknown, but to bring about the re-birth of a Jewish state. This movement is known as the Zionist Movement.

The first Jews to make this modern return came to the land of Israel, Palestine as it was then called, as early as 1878, to found a village which they named Petah Tikvah (Gate of Hope). By 1882 other small groups of Zionists, also from Russia and Poland, who called themselves 'Hovevei Zion' (Lovers of Zion) had arrived in the country with the sole aim of reclaiming and farming what over the centuries had become desolate wastelands. The pogroms in Russia, often perpetrated in the name of Christ, had made it unsafe for any Jewish family to live even in those areas of Russia where they were technically permitted. The vital necessity of a Jewish homeland was vividly apparent and thus began the first Aliyah (going up) to Palestine, the land of Israel. Meanwhile in Paris, Theodore Herzl, quite unaware of what was happening to his fellow Jews in Eastern Europe, or of the existence of the Hovevei Zion, became deeply perturbed by the infamous Dreyfus trial in 1894. As the correspondent in Paris of an important Vienna newspaper, Herzl was assigned to cover the trial of Captain Dreyfus, a Jewish officer in the French Army at the time of the Franco-Prussian War. Shocked by the injustice done to Dreyfus and by the open anti-Semitism in France, Herzl became not only interested in the fate of his people, but convinced that there was only one possible and permanent answer, namely a return to Palestine and the formation of a Jewish state. He consequently became the prophet of Zionism and the founder of the World Zionist Organization.

Today, it is quite common for anyone, be they Jew or Gentile, to be called a Zionist, simply because they believe in the right of the state of Israel to exist and therefore wish to participate in her future.

2.   THE PALESTINIAN REFUGEE PROBLEM

Much is now heard about the rights of the Palestinian refugee. The facts that lie behind the problem are not widely known. What has registered in Western minds has been the vociferous voices of the Arab leaders, both national and terrorist and the harsh fact that the world's major oil deposits on which the economies of the West depend, lie in Arab hands.

It is an interesting fact that the early Arab nationalists never referred to the Palestinians as such or to their rights. In May 1947 their argument at the U.N. General Assembly was that 'Palestine was part of the province of Syria' and that 'politically the Arabs of Palestine were not independent in the sense of forming a separate political entity'. As late as May 31st, 1956, Ahmed Shukairy, the Saudi Arabian delegate to the U.N. (and later the leader of the Palestinian Liberation Organization) told the Security Council 'It is common knowledge that Palestine is nothing but Southern Syria'. The Palestinian refugee came into being in 1948, but to talk about the Palestinian and his rights only became convenient for Arab nationalists as a political weapon against Israel in more recent years.

The Palestinian Arab before 1948. Until the growth of Jewish immigration to Palestine at the beginning of this century and the resulting increase in prosperity, Palestine was a place of Arab emigration. Large areas of land were owned either by absentee landlords or by local sheiks and the Palestinian Arab was usually in their debt. He consequently suffered most from the hand of his fellow Arab and at the best earned for himself and his family a very meagre existence. Bedouin bands frequently roamed and plundered their villages and as a result many were leaving Palestine for Trans-Jordan and elsewhere.

Then came the Jewish pioneers. Great tracts of the country had for centuries remained in an arid or semi-arid condition. Huge areas were only malarial swamp. It was usually these areas that the Jews bought, often at exhorbitant prices and then began to transform. Arid land became fertile, malarial swamps were drained, prosperity from the land became a reality and then the Palestinian Arab wanted to join in. From 1922 Arab emigration turned to one of immigration. From Syria, Iraq, Lebanon, Trans-Jordan and Egypt they began to migrate to Palestine. Between the two world wars the increase was extraordinary, notably in the areas of Jewish concentration and development. In Haifa for example, the Arab population during these years increased two hundred and sixteen per cent as against thirty-two per cent in Bethlehem or forty-two per cent in Nablus. The British Royal Commission of 1937 clearly related the rapid increase in the Arab population of Palestine (565,000 in 1922; 1,200,000 by 1947) to the Jewish presence, for it was in stark contrast to the record of other Arab countries, notably Trans-Jordan.

Why then did the Palestinian leave? Until the creation of a Jewish state in 1947, the Arab was coming into the land. Why then did they leave in

1948? Many contradictory statements have been made as to the causes. Israeli spokesmen point to a number of contributory causes and one overwhelming reason. A substantial proportion of the Palestinian Arab middle and professional classes emigrated voluntarily with much of their property, prior to the foundation of the state of Israel and have settled happily elsewhere. Many Arab villagers and peasants left because their leaders had deserted them. A small percentage left directly as a result of the 1948 war, especially around Ramleh and Lydda, where the Israeli army was forced to bring about their evacuation. Then came the tragic massacre at Deir Yassin, an Arab village a few miles to the south-west of Jerusalem and an area of much fighting which had a profound effect on Arab morale. On April 8th, 1948, a patrol of the Jewish para-military organization Irgun Zvi Leumi attacked the village in the course of which two hundred and fifty-four Palestinian men women and children were killed. The Irgun claimed that the villagers put out white flags and then opened fire on them, killing eight and wounding fifty-seven. The Israeli Government of Ben Gurrion publicly deplored the incident and they in any case disliked the Irgun whom they regarded as an illegal organization. Whatever the truth is behind the massacre, there is no doubt that its story, fanned by Arab propaganda, induced many Arabs to flee from their homes in other parts of Palestine. While in no way wishing to excuse this act, it is only right to point out that it was more than matched by Arab atrocities upon Jewish communities.

The overwhelming reason however for the Palestinian leaving the country was simply that of Arab hostilities and propaganda. There would have been no refugee problem if the leaders of the Arab states, notably Egypt, Syria and Jordan, had not declared war on the new state of Israel and then urged their Palestinian kinsmen to either join in the battle, or to evacuate Israel and return after the Arab armies had destroyed the Jews. A good example of the effect it had is seen in Haifa. Due to Jewish immigration, the city had grown and prospered enormously and was the major port in the land. Outside of Jerusalem, Haifa was the biggest Jewish-Arab community in Palestine and the two communities lived in security and harmony up until 1948. The Arab states then broadcast to them to leave prior to the Arab invasion and intimated that those who stayed accepting Jewish protection would be regarded as renegades. On the other hand the leaders of the Jewish municipality pleaded with them to stay and serve as an example throughout the land that Jews and Arabs could continue to live together in harmony. However, of the 62,000 Arabs who formerly lived in Haifa not more than 6,000 remained. It was essentially Arab propaganda and Arab hostilities that put it into the minds of the Arabs of Palestine to leave that land.

The Arab case is the simple yet deceptive argument that the Jews deliberately drove out thousands of Palestinians from their homes in a campaign of ruthlessness and brutality. Even the most moderate Arab spokesmen accept this explanation. Apart from Deir Yassin, the evidence however does not bear them out, neither do their own admittances in 1948 and onwards. For example:

Emile Ghoury, Secretary of the Palestinian Arab Higher Committee, in an interview with the Beirut Telegraph (Sept. 6, 1948):
'The fact that there are these refugees is the direct consequence of the act

of the Arab states in opposing partition and the Jewish state. The Arab states agreed upon this policy unanimously and they must share in the solution of the problem.'

The Jordanian daily newspaper Falastin (Feb. 19, 1949):
'The Arab states which had encouraged the Palestine Arabs to leave their homes temporarily in order to be out of the way of the Arab invasion armies, have failed to keep their promise to help these refugees'.

Kul-Shay, Moslem weekly (Beirut, Aug. 19, 1951):
'Who brought the Palestinians to Lebanon as refugees, suffering now from the malign attitude of newspapers and communal leaders, who have neither honour nor conscience? Who brought them over in dire straits and penniless, after they lost their honour? The Arab states, and Lebanon amongst them, did it.'

The Cairo daily – Akhbar el Yom (Oct. 12, 1963):
'The 15th May, 1948, arrived ... On that day the Mufti of Jerusalem appealed to the Arabs of Palestine to leave the country, because the Arab armies were about to enter and fight in their stead.'

In 1953, April 9, the Jordanian daily newspaper Al Urdun:
'For the flight and fall of the other villages it is our leaders who are responsible because of their dissemination of rumours exaggerating Jewish crimes and describing them as atrocities in order to inflame the Arabs ... By spreading rumours of Jewish atrocities, killings of women and children etc. they instilled fear and terror in the hearts of the Arabs in Palestine, until they fled leaving their homes and properties to the enemy.'

No wonder even the Soviet delegate in the Security Council on March 4th, 1949, said in the debate on the Arab refugee problem, 'Why should the state of Israel be blamed for the existence of that problem?'

How many Palestinian refugees are there? There are conflicting estimates ranging from 500,000 to 2,000,000. The usual Arab claims are for 900,000 refugees at the end of 1949, one and a half million by the mid sixties, and over two million by 1974.

At the beginning of the period of large scale immigration and before the British Mandate, the Arab population of Palestine was certainly under 1,000,000, and was decreasing. According to official British figures it had risen from a low point in the 1920's to 1,200,000 by 1947. Of the 1,200,000, 450,000 lived in areas that did not become part of the state of Israel after the truce in 1949. (Some estimates put the figure at 550,000 or more.) Of the remaining 750,000 Arabs, about 160,000 either remained in their homes or returned soon after the fighting ended. The number of Palestinian Arab refugees displaced in 1947–48 was therefore at the most 600,000.

The United Nations Economic Survey Commission (UNESCOM) put the figure at 726,000 in 1949, but reported that the number of bogus refugees on their lists was as high as 160,000. Prior to January 1950, the U.N. was actually producing rations for 940,000 and voluntary agencies were feeding another 79,000. By May 1950, when all refugee administration was placed in the hands of U.N.R.W.A. (Relief and Work Agency for Palestinian Refugees), it inherited a roll of 957,000 and by 1967 it was up to 1,344,576. However U.N.R.W.A. accepted the principle that any child of a refugee could also be registered. By 1970 more than half the Palestinian Arabs with refugee status had been born in exile.

The majority of the Palestinian refugees fled into Trans-Jordan for they had relatives there. As Jordan was a very poor country, friends and relatives who were not refugees at all, were amongst the applicants for U.N. relief. U.N. officials found it hard if not impossible, to distinguish between the various applicants, chiefly because of the similarity of names. Furthermore, while births in refugee families were registered by them, deaths were not.

There is also evidence for the forging of ration cards. A black market was particularly active in Gaza. U.N.R.W.A. records in the Gaza Strip in 1967 showed 312,000 refugees and 118,000 indigenous Arabs. An Israeli census after the six-day war (none there had time to leave) showed only 222,000 refugees.

The 1967 war produced a new refugee problem, the bulk of whom were from the West Bank. Some of these were 'old' refugees from the 1948–49 conflict. Again estimates differ widely. U.N.R.W.A. believed that about 175,000 'old' refugees fled for a second time. Certainly there were between 130,000 and 160,000 new refugees in 1967, but by the beginning of 1974 over 25,000 of these had returned.

What is their present plight? The generally held Arab view now is that all Palestinian refugees, their children and their offspring have the right to return to the old homes, since the whole of Palestine including the state of Israel, is the property of the Palestinian people. Only those Jews whose families had been settled in Palestine before 1917 should really be allowed to remain. The Israeli view is that any general repatriation of the refugee (they have already allowed thousands to return) is dependent upon the establishment of peace.

The Arab Governments have deliberately maintained the miserable plight of the refugee as a propaganda weapon against Israel. Approximately two-fifths of the refugees have settled in Jordan, one-fifth in Syria and Lebanon and one-fifth are in Israel, seventy per cent of whom are no longer in camps. The rest have been assimilated throughout the Arab world as well as in Europe and America. Generally speaking the worst off refugees are those still living in the camps of Jordan, Syria and Lebanon. The civil wars in Jordan in 1970 and more recently in Lebanon have centred around these camps for they have been the centre of terrorist activities. In Syria many are recruited into their para-military force for guerrilla activities along Israeli borders. Refugee children have been systematically taught to hate Israel and its people and U.N.R.W.A. has been unable to prevent this political indoctrination. Today something over one and a half million Palestinian Arabs claim refugee status and about 800,000 of these draw U.N.R.W.A. food rations. Over 400,000 still live in camps and often in miserable conditions. The Arab countries' contribution towards the financing of U.N.R.W.A., has been pitiable. The United States has contributed seventy per cent of the funds, Britain's contribution is second largest and France and Canada have also made substantial contributions together with Sweden. Israeli contributions have been on a higher scale than any of her Arab neighbours. The Soviet Union and the Soviet bloc have contributed nothing at all. So whereas the six Western powers, chiefly the United States have given three hundred and fifty million pounds up to 1972, the total contribution from the five richest Arab oil states was four million pounds and the nineteen Arab states together managed only thirteen million pounds or under five per cent of U.N.R.W.A.'s regular expenditure. The Arab Governments have consistently rejected any move to resettle these refugees anywhere in the Arab world. With a reasonable degree of co-operation from the Arabs as many as 400,000 refugees could have been resettled in the 1950's. Human needs have been subordinated to political considerations, so preventing any genuine progress towards the solution of a problem that has caused and is still causing, unnecessary human suffering.

The Problem in Focus. The Arab exodus from Palestine is only the 12th largest movement of refugees to take place since the end of World War II. The India-Pakistan conflict for example led to 2,388,000 Moslems moving from India into Pakistan and 2,644,000 Hindus moving from Pakistan to India. Official West German statistics show that by September 1950 almost exactly three million Sudeten Germans had been expelled from Czechoslovakia. Of these 916,000 had settled in E. Germany and the remainder in W. Germany and Austria. The total number of refugees from East Germany is more than three and a half million, and six and three-quarter million Germans left their homes in the provinces annexed by Poland. More recently we have had the refugees of the Nigerian civil war. Although figures are less precise, there were at least two million Ibo refugees. When Vietnam was partitioned, 800,000 North Vietnamese moved to the South. In Korea the same thing happened with approximately the same numbers involved. The recent settlement of the refugees from South Vietnam into other parts of the world ran into thousands. The number of refugees from China that have come to Hong Kong are reckoned to be over one million, although little is said about this for obvious diplomatic reasons. Today we have still to learn the full number of refugees as a result of the war in Angola.

Furthermore we do well to remember that the exodus of Jews from Arab lands since 1948 has been even larger than the flight of Arabs from Israel or Palestine. In 1948 there were almost 850,000 Jews in Arab lands, from Morocco to Iraq. By 1973 there were less than 50,000. Many of them came to Israel with only the clothes they stood up in. In Baghdad alone the Iraq Government in 1951 confiscated thirty-five million pounds in cash from Jewish accounts in banks. In Egypt an estimated three hundred and fifty million pounds of property was left behind by Jewish refugees. Yet all these refugees have been absorbed into Israel, despite the many thousands of Jewish immigrants from elsewhere. Israel has solved her Jewish refugee problem from Arab lands despite having less wealth and resources and with other enormous problems to solve. Moreover she has settled and rehoused seventy per cent of the Arab refugees within her borders. She would welcome home the remaining 50,000 Jews in Arab countries were they all free to come.

Whereas every one of the non-Arab countries that received a flood of refugees did their best to settle the new arrivals, the strenuous efforts of the

Arab countries has been to prevent or limit such resettlement. The reason for this callousness is simple and is avowedly political. If the Arab refugees were to find new jobs and homes in Syria, Lebanon, Jordan and Egypt, they might too easily settle down and lose their sense of Palestinian identity and yearning for their old homes, which has been kept alive through continuing lies and propaganda. For this reason alone the Arab Governments have denounced and thwarted all international attempts to resettle the refugees in lands away from Israel's borders.

3. THE DILEMMA FOR THE PALESTINIAN

I do not know of any country as young or as small as Israel where there is so much humanitarian concern and goodwill for others, particularly towards the undeveloped countries of the so-called Third World. The enthusiastic help that Israel has been willing to give to a number of African countries and to some in South America, has been truly remarkable. This has notably been by way of technical advice and help given in land reclamation, in medicine and public health, in engineering, in regional planning and in a host of other fields. It has been part and parcel of the ideals of Zionism. If such help is anything to go by, the goodwill and assistance they would be willing to give to their Arab neighbours should be something to marvel at. No wonder King Abdullah of Jordan, King Hussein's grandfather, said not long before his assassination, that he believed the return to the Middle East of the Jewish people could be nothing but blessing for the Arab peoples. Indeed he believed that Providence had dispersed the Jews throughout the Western World in order that they might absorb European culture and technology and bring it back with them to the Middle East, thus creating a new chapter for the Semitic peoples.

However no one, least of all the Israelis, would say that every decision and action by the Israeli Government had been good and right, any more than one could say this of the British or American Governments. Indeed, it would be nothing short of a miracle if the Israeli Government had been unerringly right for all of the last twenty-eight years. While there may have been some unfortunate actions, the main direction of Israeli policy has been both humanitarian and righteous. When however we clear away the misunderstanding, the misinterpretation and the distortion of the facts which have characterized the Middle East situation and particularly the Arab attitudes, we are left with a real bedrock problem. That problem is the future for the Palestinian. Despite the fact that Arab members of Parliament sit in the Knesset (Israel's Parliament); that Arab towns have their own mayors and councillors; that Arab students are able to go for their university studies to Cairo or Beirut; that the Jordan bridges are open to residents of the West Bank; that forty-seven clinics have been established on the West Bank giving a free service; that the standard of living has risen enormously (despite the inflation), despite all this and much more, the fact still remains that the Palestinian Arab finds himself a second class citizen. Above all, it is the impossibility of ever attaining a top position in industry, commerce and other fields of national importance, including high office of state, that makes the Palestinian Arab feel a second class citizen in Israel. Indeed, the more he enjoys all these other privileges, the more this feeling of being a second class citizen becomes apparent. Quite naturally the Palestinian Arab wants to be totally in charge of his own destiny.

Yet what can Israel do? Can she afford to permit an Arab to become Minister of Defence, or join the army, or control a vital sector of the economy? Maybe in time such a possibility will become a reality, but no Jewish Israeli feels such a time has yet come. Furthermore, to allow another Arab state to exist within the present borders of Israel would be military suicide for the Jewish state. To return to the borders of 1967, with Israel only twelve miles wide and her Parliament within one mile of the border, would be ridiculous. Yet no matter how enlightened an Israeli administration is, the dilemma for the Palestinian Arab remains. While the purpose of this book has not been to answer this particular problem in depth, it is only right to point out, that this is a very real problem.

The answer is undoubtedly for the breakdown of all the distrust, misunderstanding and bitterness on both sides and this will take much time. The first step must be the recognition of the state of Israel on the part of the Arabs. From such a genuine and whole-hearted recognition tremendous blessing and enrichment would come to the whole Middle East, and not least to the Palestinian.

Glossary

Day of Atonement

The Day of Atonement as originally commanded by God is fully described in the pages of the Old Testament. See such passages as Leviticus 16:29–34; 23:26–32; and 25:9. During the ceremony of the day, two goats were presented before the Lord. One goat was slain and its blood was sprinkled before the Mercy Seat by the High Priest, this being the only day of the year he was able to enter into the Holy of Holies. He then prayed over the other goat and by laying his hands on the animal God thereby transferred the sins of the nation to the goat, which was then led out of the temple to the edge of the wilderness to carry its awesome burden out of sight. It was therefore known as the scapegoat. In this manner atonement was made for the sins of the Children of Israel once every year.

With the destruction of the temple in Seventy A.D. and the dispersion of the Jewish people, observation of the Day of Atonement was no longer possible in accordance with the Levitical law. Instead Jewry has sought to maintain it in spirit, and has therefore right through the Dispersion (the Diaspora) observed it as the holiest day of the year, a day to·be spent preferably in the synagogue, in prayer and total fasting. It is a day of repentance before God. With the establishment of the state of Israel the day has been nationally observed in the same manner and since 1967 and the taking of the Old City of Jerusalem, the rams horn (shofar) is again sounded at the Western or Wailing Wall (Lev. 25:9).

For the Christian this day also has tremendous meaning in an understanding of the work of Jesus Christ on the Cross. See for example Hebrews 9:11–14; 24–26 and Hebrews 10:19–22.

The Book of the Living

During the Old Testament days and probably long afterwards, Jewish authorities kept a register of the names of those living within their communities. When a person died his name was blotted out from the record for it only contained the names of the living. It is an ancient Jewish tradition that God keeps such a book in heaven and that each man's destiny is based upon his name being entered there or otherwise.

Armageddon

Armageddon is the Greek form of the Hebrew Har-Megiddo which literally means 'The Mountain of Megiddo'. Megiddo was a fortress city in the plain of Jezreel also known as the plain of Esdraelon, at the north-east of Mount Carmel and is mentioned several times in the Old Testament (see for example Joshua 17:11; II Kings 9:27; II Chron. 35:22; Zech. 12:11.). Its remains are with us to this day. Megiddo dominated the vast plain of Jezreel, a plain which has been the battleground between the different super powers throughout recorded history, from the Assyrian-Egyptian rivalries to the final defeat of the Turks there by General Allenby in World War I. It is because John, in the book of Revelation, speaks of the kings of the whole world being gathered together at Armageddon to war against God, that Christians consider it to be the literal place on earth where at the end of human history, the leaders of this world will be utterly defeated in an actual battle by the armies of the Lord Jesus Christ.

The Jewish Agency

The Jewish Agency is an international non-government body, centred in Jerusalem. For most of its life it has been the executive and representative of the World Zionist Organization. Its aims have always been to assist and encourage Jews throughout the world to help in the development and settlement of what was originally Palestine and is now Israel. After the First World War, with the League of Nations Mandate for Palestine, it was recognized by that body as the appropriate Jewish public body 'for the purpose of advising and co-operating with the administration of Palestine in such economic, social and other matters as may affect the establishment of the Jewish National Home and the interests of the Jewish population in Palestine.'

Between the two World Wars the Jewish Agency was responsible for organizing political pressure in Britain with respect to the administration of Palestine under the Mandate; for supervising the clandestine Jewish defence force (the Haganah) which in turn became the basis of the Israeli Army; for obtaining the legal immigration of Jews from Germany in the 1930's and indeed from throughout Europe; for arranging the Youth Aliyah programme designed to bring out children from Nazi Germany, and through its fund-raising organization (Keren Hayesod) for economically developing the land of Israel.

During the Second World War it fought the White Paper restrictions on land purchase and immigration mainly by organizing 'illegal' immigration of survivors from Europe in the face of determined British opposition. At the same time the Jewish Agency took the lead in mobilizing the resources of world Jewry on behalf of the Allied War effort. David Ben-Gurion, chairman of the executive of the Jewish Agency from 1935, called on Jews everywhere to fight the British Government's restrictions as if there were no War, and to fight the War as if there were no restrictions.

With the Allied victory and disclosure of the full horror of the Nazi holocaust, the Agency was in the forefront in the struggle for a Jewish state. This mainly involved its members in disputes with the British authorities in Palestine and in June 1946, several of its executive members were arrested.

In New York it was the Jewish Agency that stated the Jewish case to the Anglo-American Commission of Enquiry of 1946 and later to the U.N. Special Committee on Palestine. Several committee members of the Jewish Agency were members of the National Council which with the declaration of independence, became the new state of Israel's provisional legislature and government, with David Ben-Gurion at its head.

After 1948 the Agency continued to deal with immigration to Israel, with the absorption of immigrants, land settlement and with the channelling of world-Jewry's support to the state. The Youth Aliyah programme adapted itself to the new conditions by providing decent homes and education for children of poor immigrant families. In several fields of education the Jewish Agency is prominent. From October 1948 to May 1963 the Jewish Agency received over £600,000,000, eighty per cent of which came from the U.S.A. After 1967 donations from world Jewry increased rapidly, enabling the Jewish Agency to finance costs of welfare and other services on behalf of immigrants hitherto borne by the Israeli Government. The United Jewish Appeal, the more recent charity fund-raising body in the U.S.A. also channels its funds to Israel through the Jewish Agency.

Since 1969 the structure and function of the Jewish Agency and the World Zionist Organization have become more distinct, as at their beginnings at the turn of the century. The Jewish Agency now deals only with 'practical' work in Israel and leaves to the World Zionist Organization the task of fostering Zionism, education, and organizational tasks in the Diaspora. The two however are still closely linked by way of membership and organization.

The Rapture

The hope of Christians today is not death but the second coming of Christ. They look forward to meeting him in the clouds of the air and for this they patiently wait. This hope rests on such Scriptures as the following:

> 'The Lord himself will come down from heaven with a mighty shout and the soul-stirring cry of the archangel and the great trumpet-call of God. And believers who are dead will be the first to rise to meet the Lord. Then we who are still alive and remain on the earth will be caught up with them in the clouds to meet the Lord in the air . . .'

> 1 Thessalonians 4:16–17
> The Living Bible.

> 'Our homeland is in heaven where our Saviour the Lord Jesus Christ is; and we are looking forward to his return from there. When he comes back he will take these dying bodies of ours and change them into glorious bodies like his own . . .'

> Philippians 3:20–21.
> The Living Bible.

It will be seen that those who sleep are raised from the dead and the living are translated. Their bodies are changed from natural to spiritual bodies being fashioned like Christ's glorious body.

This event is known as 'the Rapture' for this conveys the meaning of 'being seized and carried away in extreme delight and ecstasy.'

The Millennium

Many believe that some time in the future and after the Rapture,
Christians will become associated with Christ in his royalty and will reign
with him on earth for a thousand years. The view is based on a number of
scriptures, the main one being:

> 'Blessed and holy are those who share in the first resurrection. For
> them the Second Death holds no terrors, for they will be priests of God
> and of Christ and shall reign with him a thousand years.'

Revelation 20:6
The Living Bible.

This period of history is known as 'the Millennium' and those who hold this
view believe that during this time Satan will be bound and imprisoned, the
mists of ignorance and superstition will be driven away and the curse which
sin brought upon the earth will be removed. Christ will reign with his own
from Jerusalem. It will be a time of perfect government, permanent peace
and unbounded prosperity with even the animal creation sharing in the
blessing. Holiness will no longer be the narrow way but the highway for
mankind. The Millennium however will still be imperfect having latent in it
the seeds which will develop into the final rebellion after Satan has been
loosed. This will be followed by the final defeat of Satan and all evil.

The Hassids

This is a religious movement that originated in parts of the Ukraine and
Poland in the 18th Century. Its followers put a great emphasis on the
outward manifestations of religious joy and ecstasy, as well as on a strict
observance of the law in its every detail. They have had a great influence
upon the course of Judaism beyond all proportion to their number. The
Hassids are quite distinctive in dress and appearance, and tend to live in
close proximity to one another. Most people recognize them by their long
side curls and wide brimmed hats trimmed with fur.

The Pogroms

This derives from a Russian word meaning 'destruction' or 'devastation'.
The word is now used to describe an organized massacre such as the
Russian Jews suffered in the late 19th and early 20th Centuries.